The Lowlands

Scotland
Art in Scotland
Scottish Crafts
The Young Traveller in Scotland
A History of Scottish Gold and Silver Work
The Lothians
The Highlands
The Young Robert Louis Stevenson

1 (overleaf)   Pittenweem Harbour, Fife

The Lowlands

Ian Finlay

HASTINGS HOUSE, PUBLISHERS
New York, 10022

Contents

The Illustrations

The Illustrations

Acknowledgment

The Author and Publishers would like to thank the following for permission to reproduce the illustrations appearing in this book:

The late Robert M. Adam, for fig. 7
G. Douglas Bolton, for figs. 1, 4–6, 10, 20, 22 and 23
J. Allan Cash, for figs. 17 and 26–9
Noel Habgood, for figs. 3, 9, 25 and 32
A. F. Kersting, for figs. 11, 12, 15, 16, 30 and 31
The *Scottish Field*, for figs. 19, 21 and 24
The Scottish Tourist Board, for fig. 8
Tom Weir, for figs. 2 and 18
Reece Winstone, for fig. 14

one

Introductory

The Lowlands of Scotland are nearly as difficult to define precisely as the Highlands are. They occupy the country between the Highlands and the English Border, but the Border has wavered madly, the Celts of Strathclyde straying south beyond Cumberland and the Northumbrians as far north as the Forth. Not until the thirteenth century did the Border settle down in approximately the position it holds to-day. This purely political boundary has no obvious justification, geographical, ethnic or linguistic. Rugged and rascally men on both sides disputed and flouted and ignored it for many generations after Alexander II and Henry III agreed upon it. In fact the Lowlands, until comparatively modern times, were a battle-ground or a buffer between the Highlands and England.

Pressure of those upper and nether millstones was a major factor in consolidating the identity of this otherwise rather elusive region. Lowlanders early learned to expect no help from north or south. Watched covetously by Highland raiders and by Border rievers, they had to husband such resources as they possessed, and in the process built up a reputation for being close-fisted and hard to deal with. Economically, those resources turned out in the long run to be considerable, so that in the nineteenth and early twentieth centuries the ironmasters and shipmasters of this small, rather remote region attained world stature. Their minds were as formidable as their hand-skills, so that spiritual leaders and thinkers arose among them who made their mark on the world's thought. The man whose hand finally drew firmly that disputed border, however, and wove together the traditions and loyalties of the country north of it for all to see, so that there could be no mistaking it for an outlier of England, was neither king nor cleric nor philosopher, but a mere writer of romances whom some unhappy intellectuals of our generation sneer at and profess to find unreadable. Sir Walter Scott was to southern Scotland very much what Queen Victoria was to the Highlands, grafting what seems at times a preposterous new imagery on to roots dying from neglect. He put the 'B' in Border country and made it a bastion more redoubtable than all the efforts of the old Border barons, and gimmicks such as the livery of Border checks or Abbotsford itself have become with time as genuinely evocative as the prospect of Balmoral.

Of course, that 'Lowlands' is a complete misnomer for the portion of Scotland left over after subtraction of the Highlands scarcely needs saying. Although in the south there is nothing of the stature of Ben Nevis or the Cairngorms, most of the area is, by English standards at least, wild and hilly, and there are indeed several tops which come near to rivalling Goatfell or Suilven. And yet, if this great tract of country is not lowland, by nature neither is it like the Highlands. There are not many views even in Galloway or the Lammermuirs which a Highland eye would not at once detect as foreign to it, different in some fundamental way. What is the basic factor in this difference?

If one can probe to any one factor, it is probably the presence or absence of metamorphic rocks. Metamorphosis denotes a protean change in the nature of rocks. It is produced by fantastic temperatures which melt the rocks and, cooling, bring about crystallisation and give birth to such materials as gneiss, granite and schist. It is the outcrops of those very hard and weather-resisting rocks which lend the Highlands their dramatic outlines, ridges such as the A'chir on Arran or the Cuillin of Skye, or pinnacles like Lochnagar and the Cobbler. Where there is a Highland touch in the Lowland landscape—Merrick for example—it is there because of the presence of metamorphic rocks; but most of the Lowland heights have weathered to softer profiles.

Once upon a time the Lowlands possessed mountain masses far mightier than the Cairngorms or Ben Nevis of to-day. The gentle, rolling Pentland hills which are the background to Edinburgh were a mile high or more in past times. Why those great mountain ranges, and others, have vanished completely can be deduced from a number of features: the rolling, table-land effect of the whole area, deep scores and scratches on exposed surfaces of rocks, deep deposits of boulder-clay in the valleys. Some weighty mass has depressed the entire region until it has sunk beneath the surface of the sea, and tides, perhaps with the aid of drifting ice-packs, have scoured all eminences until they were rubbed down into the undulating hills and vales of the Border country as we know it now.

Perhaps more obvious than the absence of rugged outlines is the grassy greenness of so much of this Lowland hill-country, by comparison with the heathy browns and greys and blues of Highland hillsides. Here again the underlying rock has a good deal to do with it. This rock is of Lower Silurian period, sandstones which have weathered away into soil deep enough to maintain sheep pastures, and in the valleys rich enough to give us the fertile lands of Tweeddale, once tilled by the monks, and Moffatdale and Nithsdale, and the dairy country of Ayrshire. Even high hill-passes such as the Dalveen and the Enterkin have little of the beetling grandeur of a Highland pass. Really it is only where these southern uplands meet the sea that their bones show. The strike of the rocks is south-west and north-east, just as in the Highland region, and their underlying nature is exposed, therefore, at one end where the Lammermuirs plunge down to Dunbar and St. Abbs, and at the other where the Galloway moors dip to Kirkcudbright and Wigtown. The rather bare farming country through which the A.1 route passes inland behind St. Abbs at the coast ends abruptly in dramatic cliffs five hundred feet above the sea, and the crags and skerries and caves below reveal both the immensity of the erosive forces and sometimes unexpected points of resistance such as the porphyry fortress of St. Abbs' Head itself; while along the western coast the storms of the Irish Sea have laid bare contortions and folds of the rocks recording lateral stresses which the scoured and scrubbed surface of the land does not reveal.

The only real lowlands are in the midland valley, the broad strip of carse-lands between Forth and Clyde, between the Highlands and the Southern Uplands. If this valley were to sink only a few yards, the sea would flow in from east and west as it must have done in the not-so-remote past. This low-lying country is walled off from the Highlands along the great fault where the crystalline schists and gneisses show, and from the Southern Uplands by another line of fault, which the shales and other soft materials reveal much less dramatically. The sea has retreated considerably, even in the centuries since the Romans were here, and the emergent plain has held out more attractions for man than all the rest of Scotland put together. Along the north side is that long belt of Lower Old Red Sandstone which has broken down into good farming land from south of Tay almost to Loch Lomond. The remainder has been one great Carboniferous layer, but portions of this have sunk lower than the rest and so, escaping the planing action of ice and tides, have survived to provide the coalfields of Fife, Lothian, Lanarkshire and Ayrshire. The long vistas of the plain are interrupted by ridges such as the Sidlaws, the Ochills, the Bathgate hills and the Pentlands and by more solitary heights like the Lomonds of Fife, Salisbury Crags which tower redly behind Edinburgh, Dalmahoy Craigs and Traprain Law. Those are hard, igneous masses, relics of a volcanic age in the form of lava surviving from the throats of volcanoes which themselves have been ground out of existence by the glaciers of a subsequent Ice Age. In this great lowland belt not only coal has become available, but also iron in some quantity, and even an amount of oil where the organic residues of lakes and marshes were compressed below the shales. Here has lain almost the entire economic strength of Scotland in the past. Here has concentrated four-fifths of her population. But the riches were won crudely and the winning of them has laid waste much of what might have been the gentlest and most rural of landscapes and spattered it with unsightly little towns, gaunt rubbish tips and a tangle of communications.

If we forget about industrial waste-lands, we must own that scenic beauty in the Lowlands owes something to man, which is another point of difference between south and north. The Improvers came late in the story of Scottish agriculture, but they worked hard and earnestly and they left a great deal of Caledonia far from stern or wild. The Scot of course has been 'typed', in cinema parlance, by all who are interested in publicising him and his country, as a sort of Rob Roy tailored by one of the more discreet Edinburgh outfitters, and the inevitable background for this apparition is one of purple moors and silver lochs. Something much more bucolic would be appropriate, although it is to

2   *Loch Leven with St Cerf's Island from Benarty Hill*

be feared there would merely be a substitution of Robert Burns and the Brig o' Doon. We are not strictly concerned with scenery in this book, except in the form of illustrations. The image of the Lowlands, however, is so coloured by the tartan spectacles offered to all visitors to Scotland that a few generalised remarks may be permitted to correct this. One concerns the village. The pretty village is, as all the world knows, something one looks out for in England. It would be useless in Scotland to look for the sophisticated attractions of Broadway or Chipping Camden or some of the Devonshire hamlets; but if one comes without preconceived notions about half-timbering and thatch there are some rewarding finds. Galloway will provide something quite different from East Lothian, Ayrshire from the Border counties, and the fishing ports of Fife are quite different again. Ornamental detail, what one of Scott's characters calls 'whigmaleeries,' is not a Scottish feature and eyes accustomed to rich Continental carving may at first sight read poverty in the plainness of a Lowland cottage; but there are other qualities to be looked for which may not be obvious but, once found, are as satisfying as any amount of decoration. These are qualities of structure and texture: basic, functional qualities which help to marry a house to the landscape. Another general observation is that Scottish farming practices lend the scene a character of their own which has its special beauty. Those Lowland fields are, usually, much larger than English fields, and their scale is in keeping with the rolling hills which are seldom out of sight. But although man has done a great deal for the landscape of the region, he does not supply its dominating features as sometimes happens in parts of England where church or village or manor house may be the most interesting thing in sight. Even the wide, cultivated tracts which occur in Lothian or Berwickshire, in Fife or Ayrshire or Dumfriesshire lie comfortably in the laps of encircling hills, and many pastures in Border dales are so shaded by forest trees that they look like natural savannah.

The climate of the Lowlands has its east–west contrasts like the climate further north. The west comes in for its share of the North Atlantic Drift, which makes just those few degrees of difference to the coastal strip from Solway to Clyde, bestowing benefits which range from earlier potatoes to fuchsia hedges and banks of hydrangea and the occasional palm. The upland country in the centre and the Border

3   *The Palace, Culross*

valleys take the brunt of winter weather, because they are least influenced by the sea. Fife and the Lothians are much drier than the west
and on paper look to be favoured parts. In winter indeed they are
probably more tolerable than the Home Counties of England, because
they are a little further removed from the land-mass of the Continent;
but in summer, and early summer especially, the low rain-fall figure
(36 inches) of the Forth estuary may be mocked for weeks on end by
those sea-mists called *haars* which bring a desolate dampness to fields
and streets and set the trees dripping in the moaning air without
precipitating anything appreciable in the rain gauges! Only *haar* conditions would prompt everyone to wear mackintoshes during an
official drought. Those bleak east winds soughing up the funnel of the
Firth of Forth were the sort of thing which drove Robert Louis Stevenson to Samoa; yet in point of fact one may as often as not escape from
them into warm sun by going a mere few miles inland.

Climate and soil between them have wrought the mixed breeds of
the Lowlands into the dour, determined race which, to most of the
world, is the representative Scot. There are riches in the Lowland
earth and below it, but they are not easily come by, and getting at them
is a hardening process. Although work and war have welded the Lowlanders into having some sort of resemblance to one another, and
common interest has made them think along the same lines, broadly
speaking, for centuries, there are several races of Lowlander. The man
of Lothian is far different from the man of Galloway, the Fifer from the
Borderer, and the Clydesider from the rest. It may be true, as H. A. L.
Fisher wrote in his *A History of Europe*, that in the Middle Ages the Lowland Scot was practically indistinguishable from the Northumbrian;
but even then the Celtic element was far more potent than Fisher
allows, and the influx of Highlanders and Irish into Glasgow and the
west in recent times has given the old stock there at least a massive shot
of Celtic blood. And this area, after all, contains about one-third of the
people of Scotland. In temperament, speech and even sometimes in
appearance, the western Lowlander is distinguishable from the eastern,
who has the reputation of being less warm-blooded, particularly in
Edinburgh. Speech betrays this difference before anything else. Speech
all across Scotland from Clyde to Forth is defined as Mid-Scots, but
western Mid-Scots at its best—in Ayrshire and the upper ward of

Lanarkshire—has a distinctive softer cadence in keeping with the climate, although around Glasgow this is corrupted by outside influences and uglified by such oddities as the glottal catch, which dispenses with the letter 't' in words like butter. Pure western Mid-Scots is the dialect of Burns, and is still capable of the elegance and tenderness with which he used it. Mid-Scots in its full range is the language of the Stewart kings, of the medieval makaris (poets) and indeed until the end of the eighteenth century of the Bench also. Industry and urban sprawl have littered it with vulgarisms as they have littered the country where it is spoken with unsightliness.

What races have gone to make up the Lowland Scot? After the ice mass receded Scotland was visited and eventually colonised both from west and east. Even in the Stone Ages the western Lowlands must have been peopled mainly from Ireland, while the Lothians and Fife, flanking the great estuary of the Forth, received the round-headed 'beaker' peoples of what are now the Low Countries. At all times there must have been an influx from 'England', refugees under pressure from further south, but this influx seems to have been greatest in the centuries just previous to our era. Strong-points such as the hill-forts— Traprain Law is the site of one of the most celebrated—belonged to those Iron Age incomers, although their types of dwelling are so varied up and down the length and breadth of Scotland that it is clear they were not a single people. It would be a mistake to picture the Scotland which first enters the pages of history through Roman authors as more densely peopled and relatively sophisticated in the Lowlands as compared with a remote and savage Highland region. The fields and pastures which now enrich the Lowlands were then sodden with treacherous bogs or covered by forests and undergrowth where wolves and bears roamed. The settlements of the Picts and Scots whom Rome never finally brought to bay may have been more numerous in the far north than in the Lowland area.

'Lowland Scotland' in Roman times for practical purposes means the region between the walls of Hadrian and of Antonine. It was occupied territory for little more than a hundred years. In later chapters we will come across evidence of Roman occupancy in this place or that, but nowhere vestiges of the gracious estates and urban amenities which left the real stamp of Roman civilisation on the southern half of England.

The occupation of South Scotland was military, and sites of temples or hypocausts or the occasional sculptured stone merely indicate that the legionary and his family liked home comforts as the U.S. serviceman abroad does to-day. Or—should we say ?—liked Roman comforts, for most of the legionaries in the army of occupation had never set eyes on Rome. The Lowlands to the Romans were no more than a defence in depth against marauders from further north, against whom commanders from Agricola to Severus launched rather ineffective punitive expeditions. The very nature of the Antonine wall, built mainly of turfs, is a confession that it was regarded not as an Imperial frontier but only as an outwork.

Before A.D. 200 the Romans had withdrawn from what is now Scotland. Over the next four centuries the Lowlands were peopled by two quite different principal races. In the west were the Britons of Strathclyde, whose sway extended from Dumbarton down to Wales until pressure from eastern tribes cut off the Scottish Britons from the Welsh ones. In the east the powerful Anglian state of Northumbria ended at the Firth of Forth. These Angles might well have pushed the Celts of Strathclyde out of existence and worked their way north until Scotland had become as English as England, but in 685 they were defeated by Brude, King of the Picts, at the great battle of Nechtansmere. Between 843 and 850 the northern tide flowed strongly under Kenneth MacAlpine, who united Scots and Picts, and the Lowlands became part of the new kingdom of Alba. The position was consolidated by the defeat of Northumbria at the battle of Carham early in the eleventh century.

Scotland's centre of gravity might be said to have remained north of the Forth until the middle of the eleventh century. The event which began the swing south was the marriage of Malcolm Canmore with the Saxon princess, Margaret. Malcolm moved his capital to Dunfermline, in Fife; but more significant than the physical move was the influence exerted upon him by his wife. Numbers of southerners were attracted to the Court, or fled there from the Norman invasion. The Celtic Church, whose itinerant priesthood moving among and ministering to the people seems to have followed faithfully the teaching of Christ in this very profound respect, lost ground to the great organised Church of Rome, so much better fitted to cope with warring secular powers.

Even the six sons of Malcolm and Margaret were none of them given traditional Celtic names. The Lowlands became the heart of Scotland. The glens of the north ceased to be fastnesses into which the Scots could retreat and became dens in which a hostile Gaeltachd lurked, ready to descend upon the crops and herds; and the long sea-lochs of the west were less highways for coastal trade to the islands than avenues through which Norse corsairs could strike at the very fringes of Lowland homesteads and abbeys.

This shift to the Lowlands of Scotland's heart brought the country much more within the European orbit. The tribal Celtic social system with its personal loyalties to chief and through him to the king, chief of chiefs, gave way before the territorial system of the Normans, the feudal system which has so long survived in Scots law. Much of the Lowlands came under this system during the reign of David I, who as a young man had lived at the English court and, through his wife, had great English estates. Strong castles, for holding down the land, grew up in southern Scotland as they had done in England. Charters granting lands and recording services to be rendered for them were issued in large numbers. The arable lands of the Lowlands came more and more under tillage, and unreckoned pastures were divided into acres and ploughgates, while Latin terms like villa and carrucate crept in through the domains of abbey and monastery linked with distant Rome.

To the new masters of these Lowland lands the boundary between England and Scotland meant little. They were Anglo-Normans and many of them held fiefs in both countries. This presented a compelling opportunity to the kings of England, for whom the taking over of Scotland seemed a logical end, and when Alexander III fell to his death from the cliffs at Kinghorn in 1286, leaving no heir but the baby 'Maid of Norway', Scottish independence appeared doomed. Even when Edward I, by her death, was foiled in his plan to wed his son to the Maid of Norway he boldly proclaimed himself Lord Paramount of Scotland. The only thing which stood between Edward and the achievement of what he claimed was the stubborn common man of the Lowlands, and he was still voiceless and leaderless. Edward, with typical medieval adroitness, turned the homage done to him by Scottish kings for lands held in England into homage done to him for the kingdom of Scotland. The many eager claimants for the Scottish throne were only too ready to acknowledge Edward's claim in return for his favour, and Edward set John de Balliol up as his puppet King of the Scots. At once opposition began to form in the Lowlands. The War of Independence had begun.

Early in the war it grew clear that Scotland's main strength lay in the Lowlands. It was the country north of the Forth that became untenable by the English, but that is because the lines of communication of the English garrisons in the north were soon stretched and cut, and because the northern glens and fastnesses were beyond the reach of invaders. The men who rose to lead the resistance were in the main Lowlanders, by domicile if not ancestry. It was the Lowlands which the English dominated through their network of mote-and-bailey castles. It was the Lowlands which the English sheriffs goaded with their ruthless rule, and it was here that the English soldiery engendered hatred.

William Wallace's was not the first blow struck for Scottish freedom. All over the country there had been stirrings of resistance, sometimes led by prominent men, but the Scots failing of disunity dissipated the effort. Whether or not Wallace slew the English Sheriff of Lanark because of the beautiful Marion Bradfute, the Scoto-Norman knight of Elderslie proved to be not only a great fighter and skilled general but also a leader of men, however critically one may read the praises of Fordoun. The time was short between his victory at Stirling Brig and his defeat at Falkirk, but it showed the Scots that their fate was something for them to decide. The rivalry for the Scottish crown which had served Edward so well was suddenly ended in 1306 when the heir of the Balliol faction, the Red Comyn, was slain by Robert Bruce in the convent of the Minorite Friars in Dumfries. Bruce—another Scoto-Norman knight—had long enough cherished his rights to the throne, but his act of violence and sacrilege put him in a position from which it was hard to retreat. He hesitated no longer. He went to Scone and had himself crowned King of Scotland.

Bruce was a remarkable man. A fugitive in February of 1307, sought by the men of Galloway who wanted his blood to avenge the Red Comyn, in May of the same year at the battle of Loudoun Hill he destroyed a superior English force under the Earl of Pembroke. Elusive, shrewd, a masterly tactician both in war and politics, he always knew exactly how and where and when to bring his limited strength to bear so that, like a judo expert, he could even use an enemy's own weight to overthrow him. Certainly, Edward I died before he could come against the new Scots king, but a lesser man than Bruce would still have succumbed to the power of English arms even with Edward II as the head. Bannockburn (1314) was the repeated tale of previous skirmishes writ large. The rest of his life Bruce devoted to trying to force Edward to recognise the independence of Scotland, and he went about it with the same careful strategy. Using the Borders no longer merely as a defensive area which he could devastate to hinder the invader, but as a sally-port for carrying the war into England, he harried Northumberland and Cumberland and even dispersed his enemy's strength by invading Ireland, at the invitation of the Irish. At last, in 1328, Edward accepted Bruce's demands and recognised Scottish independence at the Treaty of Northampton, sealing the affair by giving his sister to be the wife of Bruce's son. But the real victory, and the lasting one, was the consolidation of the kingdom, the binding of the Scots into one people. With the loyalty of the Norman lords of southern Scotland committed, for the most part, to the Scottish crown, it became possible at last for the slow growth of prosperity to be fostered in the fertile Lowlands, and for the burghs and ports there to develop their trade.

A time of setback followed the death of Bruce, and inevitably the Lowlands suffered most. Materially they had not a great deal to lose. Edinburgh and Glasgow were mere villages and Froissart records the miserable standard of life in a country which had not even iron to make weapons to defend itself with except it were brought from abroad. It seemed for a time that the wisdom of Bruce had been forgotten. Small, ill-armed Scots armies challenged great English ones, as at Halidon Hill, and were obliterated. Twenty years after Bannockburn an English king had again made good his claim to suzerainty over Scotland and English garrisons and sheriffs once more ruled all the country from the Forth to the Solway. This time it took more than a century to throw them out. Scotland had some doughty fighters along her Border, men such as the great Earl of Douglas who died in the hour of victory at Otterburn; but to the bitter disappointment of their French allies they knew better than to fight great battles, and guerilla war is slow to bring results. Fortunately for Scotland, the Hundred Years War forced

Edward III and his successors to fight on two fronts. Her material resources, however, were drained by the ransom which had to be paid to
recover her useless king, David II, captured in a battle which his father
would never have been foolish enough to fight.

Stability in the Lowlands was essential to Scotland's emergence as a
nation. Only here was it possible to build up prosperity. Thirteen of
the seventeen burghs which helped to negotiate for the release of King
David come within the Lowland region as defined in this book, and
although the interest of the burghs in the government of the country
was at first limited to the raising of taxes, these burghs were the basis
of the eventual third estate. The protection of the burgh's privileges
and the fostering of their trade through the firm administration of
justice was a first step towards a stronger nation, and this James I
(1406–37) was resolved to bring about when he declared he would
'make the key keep the castle and the bracken-bush the cow'. The
romantic young man, who had described his love for Joan Beaufort in
The Kingis Quair, took the strongest measures with his unruly nobles;
brought to heel the great Lord of the Isles and so gained the respect of
the Highlands; made the law take action even for his humblest subjects
and exhorted the Church to do its duty towards the poor if it were to
expect his protection. He roused hatred and paid for it with his life;
but he laid the foundations for better things, and saw the foundation of
the first of the Scottish universities, St. Andrews. And even with his
death at Perth the last strand of the traditional bond between the royal
authority and the Highlands was broken, for the child James II was
crowned not at Scone, but in Edinburgh, in the chapel of Holyrood.
When the new King mastered the south by slaying the Earl of Douglas
and defeating his brothers in battle, Scotland came another step nearer
to effective nationhood. This was brilliantly attained under James IV
(1488–1513). If we cannot believe all the Spanish envoy, Pedro de
Ayala, says of the Scotland of this reign, we can accept enough together with known historical fact to know that the country enjoyed
something like a little 'Elizabethan Age'. Under a court celebrated for
its chivalry, protected well both by land and sea, Scotland developed
her skills and her commerce, lived on the whole well and bred some
excellent poets. The King, unhappily, was quixotic, and the glories of
his reign ended unnecessarily on the field of Flodden.

There was no divine right of kingship in Scotland. The relationship of Crown to commons had been defined as early as the Declaration of Arbroath, in Bruce's reign. The democratic tradition which Scotland built up through the centuries in time lent her a weight in European affairs far out of proportion to her size or economic strength, and it reflects the dominance of the Lowlands. Your Celt is a born courtier. Scottish democracy grew in the polyglot south, and especially along the coasts and estuaries where trade flourished and the power of the Third Estate increased until it could challenge first Church then Crown. While the Highlands to the north and the Border barons to the south clung to medieval ways, the burgesses from Fife to Ayrshire built for the future by cultivating skills useful both in peace and war and by fostering education. They called in Frenchmen to teach them, and Flemings from the Low Countries, and the last especially came to form quite an important element in the population. The Flemings were to south-east Scotland in some respects what the exiled French Huguenots were to south-east England after the Revocation of the Edict of Nantes in 1685.

The Reformation (1560) might never have taken place if Scotland's centre of gravity had not established itself in the Lowlands. Although the nobles guided the movement, the mood which made it possible grew out of the burgesses and merchants and there was strong sympathy for it in east coast ports where, of course, influence of the Low Countries was very strong. The Highlands remained a stronghold of Roman Catholicism, and even Aberdeen remained reactionary for generations. It is not without significance that John Knox was Lothians-born, and all the straws in the wind of change, from Lyndsay's satirical play *The Three Estates* to the burning of George Wishart and Patrick Hamilton, blew around that draughty estuary of the Forth whose climate has already had mention. It was through Leith and other east coast ports that Luther's doctrines and Tyndale's translation of the New Testament had been coming in. It was in St. Andrews that Cardinal Beaton was slain to avenge Wishart. The climax came with the English invasion of 1547, which compelled a renewal of the 'auld alliance' between Scotland and France. French pressure duly brought about the withdrawal of the English army, but the marriage of the young Mary Queen of Scots to the Dauphin Francis gave promise of an absentee queen and the reduction of Scotland to being a province of France. When the Reformers came together as the Army of the Congregation of Christ Jesus, France and Catholicism were their enemies. The Treaty of Edinburgh (1560) inaugurated a new era by ending the 'auld alliance', making a gesture towards England by abjuring Mary's claim to the English throne; and—although religion had no mention—it cleared the path for the Reformation. Mary re-entered her homeland through the port of Leith. She was going into the very fortress of embattled Protestantism. Knox was quick to proclaim that 'the very face of heaven' was dolorous, and the six short years of her rule in Scotland gave her small comfort.

By the end of the sixteenth century Edinburgh as capital had grown to her full stature. Here centred the struggle between Kirk and Crown which James VI pursued with more subtlety than his mother had employed. Knox's successor was Andrew Melville. He developed the organisation of the Kirk on more and more democratic lines and indeed its General Assembly came to mean more to Scotland than her parliaments did; but the astute King used Edinburgh as a lever for his will, and by threatening to remove from the city Court and Privy Council and Law Courts he forced the Assembly to introduce a form of bishop. Scotland was anxious for her law system, as for her Kirk, and Edinburgh's vulnerability as the focal point of Scottish institutions has even to this day made her specially jealous for their retention. James returned only once to his former capital, despite his promises. Charles I had none of his father's guile. His attempts to impose episcopacy on the Lowlands—for the Highlands and the north-east were with him—consolidated opposition and brought about the National Covenant of 1638. In Glasgow the General Assembly refused to be dissolved and proceeded to excommunicate Charles's 'bishops'. The Covenanters' War had begun. It was the beginning of Charles's downfall. But in the years that followed all southern Scotland bled with the bitter struggle in which men were hunted down for their faith, but a faith which hardened them into committing terrible deeds in its name.

Scotland as a whole had small material benefit from the Union of the Crowns. At first even the Lowlands remained poor by English standards. Agriculture was backward and continued so until the eighteenth century. Beef cattle and timber were imported from the Highlands. There were exports, but not of manufactured goods, and so there was a chronic crisis in balance of payments, and only during Cromwell's ascendancy did the partner England lower her tariffs. One region of Scotland, however, did prosper steadily after 1603. Glasgow was well placed for trading with the American plantations, and she even defied the English Navigation Act, so that the sugar importers and the 'Tobacco Lords' built up respectable fortunes, and the town doubled in size long before 1700. Progress in the rest of the Lowlands lagged far behind this, but there was a spread of manufactures. Woollens, linen, even silk-weaving were among them. And so by the early years of the eighteenth century the Lowlands had successfully bent the determination hitherto dedicated to war and to religious disputation towards the end of industry and commerce, and in Edinburgh and Glasgow the state of the craft guilds at this time shows that the standard of living had attained a fair level.

It is scarcely surprising that in the Jacobite adventures of the 'Fifteen and the 'Forty-five the Lowlands took up a standpoint very different from that of the north. Roman Catholic and Episcopal sympathies in the north roused a good deal of enthusiasm for the Stewart cause in parts of the Highlands; whereas the strongly Reformed Lowlands, with their extremist Covenanting elements, saw nothing but danger in the possibility of a return of the Stewart dynasty. No less strong an influence in swaying the Lowlands against any adventurous policy was the economic one. Scotland's agricultural and industrial needs required peace for their development, and when Prince Charles looked for 10.000 men to rally to him in Edinburgh only 300 came forward.

When Culloden ended the threat to their peace the Lowlands at last began completely to dominate the pages of Scottish history. The Agricultural Revolution, already begun, and then the Industrial Revolution, changed the outward appearance of the country. By the end of the century Lowlanders had increased ten-fold the value of their lands. The potentially rich soils of coastal belts and inland straths and valleys were drained and enriched and turned into something like the ordered beauty which they retain to-day, and they were sprinkled with farm-houses and mansions. But where massive deposits of coal and iron had lain hidden a greedy onslaught was made upon these resources, and the blight of giant chimneys and belts of acrid smoke and bings of waste material made hideous wide areas which have never recovered from

the assault on their virgin beauty. A more natural and gracious industrial development was the spread of textile manufactures which
dotted the course of every stream capable of yielding water-power
with mills, large and small: linen, cotton, coarser fabrics and those
woollens which, in the Borders with their romantic association with
Scott, came to be called tweeds. Printing, sugar-refining, distilling and
brewing, rope-making and a hundred lesser trades were added to the
basic industries. The chains of towns grew which, in our own day, are
merging in what we know as 'conurbations'; but until well into the
nineteenth century the Lowlands held a reasonably happy balance between town and country, and it is not until the beginning of Victoria's
reign that Lowland Scotland's population began to be dominantly urban.

The effect of all this on the industrial towns and cities will come out
in later chapters. Now it need only be said that the stir and ferment of
the two revolutions was matched by compensations, notably vigorous
intellectual activity. At a time when Highland bards were lamenting the
sunset of past glories, Lowland clerics and scholars and poets were
enjoying the pleasures of a new sophistication. The bitter extremism
of the seventeenth century and its religious struggles waned. Before
the end of the eighteenth century a situation had arisen in which a
sceptic like David Hume roused the Kirk, not so much to denunciation
as to eager disputatiousness. Under the sway of the Moderates the Kirk
had lost its Knoxian fire. It found it again, but not until the dark satanic
mills of nineteenth-century industrialism brought out again some of the
Lowlander's grimmer aspects. Robert Burns, it is true, repeatedly
came under the severe displeasure of a Calvinist Kirk; but the same
Robert Burns knew what it felt like to be lionised by Edinburgh society.
Burns is essentially the poet of that hard-working, striving, thinking
Lowland Scotland, with its growing political awareness, at a time when
Highland poets were still spending their gifts on romanticising the
Prince who had impetuously sacrificed their forebears to butchery at
the hands of redcoats. If Burns openly taunted the reigning monarch as
'a wee German lairdie', his purpose was not to sigh after Jacobitism
but to preach the brotherhood of man. He was a man of his times. The
Lowlands which bred him were contributing to a revolution much
more widespread and profound than the Terror which had Paris in its
grip.

The intellectual flowering of Scotland in the eighteenth and early nineteenth centuries was, indeed, almost entirely a Lowland phenomenon. Burns was only one— if supreme among them—of a galaxy of poets stemming from the Lowland country stock. Allan Ramsay somewhere around 1720 had given up his wig-making to foster literature through his circulating library and to write a strain of merry verse which was to influence men like Robert Fergusson and Burns himself. There grew up a new period of verse-making in the Lowlands, both in English and in dialect. The dialect verse sprang up spontaneous, earthy and rich with native quality until the genius of Burns compelled an element of imitation such as one finds, for example, among the weaver poets of Paisley. Versifiers in pure English, on the other hand, needed many years before they could achieve spontaneity, for the language from across the Border was not the tongue they spoke in, and we find them admitting their style 'smelled of the lamp', so that even the great David Hume, the historian Robertson and Reid the philosopher, men of international repute, worked arduously to eliminate every trace of what they felt to be a 'provincial' idiom. Many of these writers, from Tobias Smollett to James Boswell of Auchinleck, took the road south and made their mark in London; but so rich were the Lowlands in talent and even genius that the capital city of Edinburgh became for a time a fount of English letters. That this should be when the language of the law-courts was still near to broad Lowland Scots is remarkable. The giant who came out of this period was Scott. Yet he was no isolated figure. Not only were there others of great ability in his circle, but the stuff of his *œuvre* was the very stuff of the Lowlands, strong, witty, wise and coming of a living oral tradition shared by a whole people. Nor was it the accident of Scott alone which made all this material available to the eager world outside Scotland, for it should be remembered that Scott was an ornament in a city and country which had its own gauntlet of informed criticism, its own flourishing background of printing and publishing and all the material apparatus of a literary renaissance.

The Lowland Scot never achieved in the visual arts the heights he achieved in literature. The word has always meant more to him than has any avenue of artistic expression, perhaps because of Knox's emphasis on the Word of God in a Kirk which had neither money nor time for those arts of which churches for centuries had been the chief patrons.

Long before the Reformation, however, poverty and remoteness from the Continent determined that building in Scotland should be on a modest scale. Quite early, Lowland valleys were colonised by the monastic orders. Abbeys and churches rose quite plentifully wherever there was good soil and pasture to be cultivated, but the buildings were slight in size by Continental or even English standards and, as a rule, much less elaborate in decoration. Romanesque remains in the Lowlands are not many, as will appear in later chapters, and often they are mere fragments among later building styles. The various phases of Gothic are much commoner, but it is characterised by marked severity, as in Glasgow Cathedral. Teams of foreign masons were responsible for a good deal of the work, but a certain rugged, dour Lowland quality distinguishes many churches, and in such an interior as St. Giles' in Edinburgh the result can be impressive. In secular building, on the other hand, Scotland borrowed from France and the Low Countries to produce a vernacular style which is at once recognisable. This emerged in the Middle Ages and gave us some notable castles, but it is in the sixteenth and seventeenth centuries that the style reached its peak. Some of the best examples are north of the Highland Line; but the Lowlands can show a great variety of town and village architecture, much of which happily is being preserved and refurbished. The eighteenth century in the Lowlands saw a wave of neo-classicism which carried on its crest the name of Robert Adam.

In painting and in the decorative arts foreign influences are again discernible from an early period. Where the craftsman of the Highlands borrowed methods and motifs from Celtic Ireland and from Scandinavia, however, the Lowlander looked to France and the Netherlands. There is not a great deal of stone or wood carving, but what there is tends to show marked Flemish influence and probably much of it was executed by Flemings who settled around the Forth estuary. The most distinguished medieval silverwork surviving is the trio of maces at the University of St. Andrews, one of them certainly made in Paris, all in the Continental 'tabernacle' form. Not until the larger burghs became prosperous did a luxury craft like goldsmithing achieve a great deal of note in the secular field, but the Kirk within half a century of the Reformation had encouraged the making of communion vessels of great beauty and dignity. Here again, in the field of silverware the eighteenth century brought neo-classicism, and Edinburgh silver of this time is in perfect accord with the Georgian New Town. In the more purely domestic realm of textiles choice craftsmanship was developed, and materials range from the linens of Dunfermline to the exquisite white needlework of Ayrshire, while under the impact of Scott the Border woollen men tried to rival the tartans of the north by producing a range of lovely checks with local associations. All those crafts grew out of the needs of increasingly prosperous communities. Painting, on the other hand, was an essentially exotic art. It had no place until the burghers attained such wealth and leisure that they took a fancy to having themselves immortalised by having their likenesses set out on 'pentit brodis'. It is to the Low Countries that Scotland turned for artists, and one of their earliest successful portrait painters, Jamesone, served his apprenticeship in a Flemish studio. Portraiture continued to be the backbone of Scottish painting until the early years of the nineteenth century, when first Allan Ramsay—son of the poet—and then Sir Henry Raeburn left splendid records of the age of the literary giants.

two

Stirling and the Carse

Stirling is at the very hub of Scottish history. It is not that more has happened here than around any other town in Scotland, but that Stirling is so centrally placed that most of the great movements in the country's history have at some time come within her horizon. She is splendidly situated. Those rich, wide, alluvial carselands of the upper Forth are dominated by the castle rock, and the military significance of that tower-topped crag breaking the back-drop of the tumbled peaks of the Perthshire Highlands is clear to anyone. In those flat lands where the Forth winds slowly eastwards any passage of men could be espied far off, whether the men were a mere few dedicated friars bearing nothing with them but their faith or whether they were an invading army with the sun glinting on its banners. This is the kind of place men have fought to hold since the earliest times.

The rock on which the Castle of Stirling is built is one of those volcanic plugs characteristic of the Forth region, rocks which have presented their western bluff to the pressure of the ice-mass and been left with a 'tail' of detritus and rock forming an easy slope to the east. Edinburgh's is the supreme example. The Rock of Stirling is nearly as perfect, and men have used it in exactly the same way, placing a citadel on its top and building a town right under the protection of this.

These strong-points sometimes meant more to the invaders than to the invaded, and in the Middle Ages it was often the English kings who built up the fortifications on the Rock of Stirling and Scots like Robert Bruce who destroyed them. Not much of the medieval Castle of

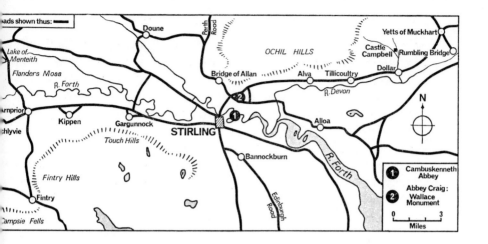

Stirling survives. The glory of the Castle buildings now is that the impact of the Renaissance upon Scotland can be seen so clearly in them, not in the form of any feeble imitation of Italian splendour but in an interpretation which is as different as Dunbar from Chaucer. The main buildings are grouped around a quadrangle: the Parliament Hall of James III, in which the medieval Gothic can be seen yielding before new ideas, the Chapel Royal, and the Royal Palace begun for James IV in 1496 and completed for James V towards the middle of the sixteenth century. Even the Palace is medieval in its basic concept, but this is forgotten in face of the extraordinary ornaments which embellish the walls. Instead of stone monsters or saints, there are on baluster columns against the walls, uncomfortably poised, figures which look as if they may well have been familiar in the streets of Stirling, perhaps even done by some local stone carver. One of them is said to represent James V himself in that guise of the 'Gudeman o' Ballengeich' in which he went among the people hereabouts. There are other sculptures of this kind, but the finest of all were the wood-carvings which once graced the ceiling of the King's presence chamber, the fifty-six splendid oaken roundels which are known as the Stirling Heads. Many of these are now dispersed and missing, as they were removed when one of them fell and injured a soldier towards the end of the eighteenth century, but several of them can still be seen preserved in the Smith Institute. These heads again show a curious blend of Renaissance elegance and local accent, and it is hard to believe they were done by the French or even Flemish artists who were attracted to the Court at this time. Traditionally, they are the work of John Drummond of Auchterarder, the King's Master-Mason, and of Andro Wood, a craftsman. Records of payments do exist showing there were carvers in Stirling who worked in the Castle. But whatever the authorship of the Heads and other carvings in wood or stone, they reflect the growing appetite of the Scots Court for the ways of the outside world, even for such exotic fancies as the keeping of lions in the so-called Lions' Den in the Palace, perhaps a quaint token of James's pride in the crown itself, that diadem which, as we shall see in another chapter, he caused to be 'casten of new' in a grander style. Indeed, the whole scale of accommodation in the Palace, modest as it may seem by comparison with French châteaux like Blois which the King may well have had in mind, is significantly more generous and luxurious than in any earlier royal residence in Scotland.

Although most of the work in the Castle dates from the end of the fifteenth century or later, Stirling for a time was practically the capital of Scotland in that the pre-Stewart kings used it for long periods as their centre. It was in the Castle that Alexander I died in 1124, and William the Lion in 1214. Alexander III fortified it against Haakon of Norway, whose threat melted away after the battle of Largs. In those days the town was known as Striviling, or sometimes Snowdon, both names with Celtic significance. With the War of Independence Stirling assumed special strategic importance for both sides, and the Castle changed hands no less than seven times in half a century. Wallace wrested it from the English after the battle of Stirling Brig (1297). They recovered it, then lost it again. In 1304 Edward I looked upon it as the greatest fortress in Scotland and laid siege to it, and when the 'Hammer' could not reduce it with his engines he stripped lead from church roofs as far off as St. Andrews to lend weight to the blows dealt by his catapults. When at last the battlements were breached the English monarch had not had an opportunity to employ his latest 'secret weapon' which he called his War-Wolf, and the besieged were not permitted to give in until this machine had demonstrated its might before the ladies of the Court, who watched from a window at a safe distance. The Castle remained in English hands until the day after the battle of Bannockburn, ten years later. In time the English retook the

4   *Stirling Castl*

place. They lost it again in 1341 when, according to Froissart, gun-powder was used in the siege, perhaps for the first time in Scotland.

The Stewarts, whose dynasty is responsible for most of the sur-viving structure, brought to Stirling Castle all the mixed pageantry and intrigue of European courts. Jousts were held on the low ground south of the Castle, presumably where the King's Park now is, and we hear of Burgundian knights matched against Scottish champions, and royally feasted afterwards by the King. We hear too of bloody executions on the Heading Hill, of the torture of the assassin of James I, the poet-king. The Parliament Hall is solid evidence of James III's preoccupation with the arts, especially architecture, which did so much to turn his nobles against him; and indeed this building could well be the work of Thomas Cochrane, one of that troupe of favourites hanged by Archibald Bell-the-Cat from Lauder Brig in 1482. James IV frequently made Stirling gay with tournaments and routs, receiving embassies, enter-taining the pretender Perkin Warbeck. On the battlements of the Castle John Damian proclaimed before a great crowd that he would be in France before the King's ambassadors and then took off by leaping from the rock, flapping the wings he had made for himself. He escaped with a broken leg and tumultuous jeers, but such was the King's interest in progress that he received him back into favour. Stirling was James V's favourite town of residence. Here he received his peasants to hear their complaints, in the garb of what he called the Gudeman o' Ballengeich, after a place just under the Castle walls. Here he brought his second wife, Mary of Guise, and the battery command-ing Stirling Brig is still known as the French Battery, possibly because it was built by French workmen brought by Mary. Her daughter, Mary Queen of Scots, regarded Edinburgh as her capital; but she often stayed in Stirling, and here in 1565 she brought her son, to be James VI, for his greater safety, and here in the Chapel Royal the baby was baptised from a golden font sent by his godmother, Elizabeth of England. But it was here too that the French Ambassador found her weeping in her chamber, distraught between her growing hatred for her husband Darnley and her awakening feelings for the Earl of Bothwell. There is a pathetic record by Sir James Melville of how the Queen led him by the hand away from the tumult of the Court down the steep streets to the Royal Park so that they could talk of the troubles of the times.

Strath Earn and the Ochil Hills

As a viewpoint, the Castle battlements are superb. The Carse spreads east and westwards, flat as a carpet, with the Forth linking its way seawards in more leisurely style than any other Scottish river. The Carse is ringed by the Campsie Fells and, to the north, by the Highland peaks and the Ochils. Every eminence has some historical significance, from the neighbouring Gowlan Hill, where Prince Charles Edward's batteries fought a losing duel with the Castle in 1746, to the distant Abbey Craig with its Wallace Tower.

Clustered in the shelter of the Castle, Old Stirling itself is full of good things. Like most Scots towns, it was miserably neglected during the nineteenth century, or smothered by tenements and commercial building; but in recent years a big effort has been made to salvage the old houses, and even to build new ones which are in keeping. It is to be hoped that this admirable spirit will be encouraged by the decision to give Stirling Scotland's newest university, for this could become a real university town in a way that large cities like Edinburgh or Glasgow could never be. I am unimpressed by the argument that a place of learning should be amongst the cut and thrust of commerce and industry, and by the same token I believe that any educational institution of such standing must benefit when surrounded by living traditions and all the necessities of a full cultural life such as theatres and museums and galleries.

Close to the gate of the Castle is the Church of the Holy Rude. Both inside and out, this is a pleasing piece of Gothic. In 1405–6 the entire town was burned down and with it the parish church. About ten years later a beginning seems to have been made with a new nave—the Chamberlain's Accounts for 1414 show that the proceeds from a court held in Stirling were devoted to the church—and even the oaken roof of this has survived. The choir was built about a century later. In 1656 the two parts were made into separate churches, the East and West Kirks, and not until 1935 did this arrangement end. There is no notable sculpture, but the detail is good and the atmosphere in keeping with the high importance of the town over many centuries. Mary Queen of Scots was crowned here as a baby, in 1543; here, a year later, her mother Mary of Guise was created Regent of the kingdom. In 1567, after a sermon by John Knox, the infant James VI was crowned in the choir, then carried back to his nursery in the Castle by the Earl of Mar. Knox preached in the church again in 1559. These events apart, the Church of the Holy Rude in its pre-Reformation days does not come prominently into the stream of history, partly no doubt because the Court worshipped in the Chapel Royal in the Castle. As a Reformed kirk, however, it had its share of doughty ministers. The Rev. James Guthrie was an indomitable Covenanter—in Cromwell's words, 'the short man who would not bow'—and suffered execution for it, his head remaining spiked on the Netherbow Port of Edinburgh for twenty eight years, despite Charles II's regard for him as an enemy of Cromwell. Another stubborn minister was Ebenezer Erskine, deposed in 1740 for defiance of the synod, the man who founded the Secession Kirk. Then in Burn's day there was that uncompromising preacher, the Rev. John Russell, of whom the poet wrote:

> His piercing words, like Highland swords,
> Divide the joints and marrow;
> His talk of Hell, whaur devils dwell,
> Our verra soul does harrow.

Opposite the Church of the Holy Rude, Broad Street turns into Castle Wynd. Here are two of the most interesting houses in Stirling. First, there is Mar's Work, or the Earl of Mar's Ludging, an unfinished residence dating from 1570, the chief interest of which is in the quaint statuary and inscriptions. Over the entrance are the Royal Arms, flanked by those of Mar and his countess. This implied link between Mar and the House of Stewart persisted until 1715, when the Earl headed the Rising. Much more impressive as a piece of architecture is the Argyll Ludging, a little way up the Wynd. Built by Sir William Alexander of Menstrie, later Earl of Stirling, around 1632, this turreted town house was taken over and added to by the Earl of Argyll. The earlier portion of the building is the finer, but in its entirety this is an outstanding example of the vernacular of the period, defaced though it was during its long years as a military hospital after 1791. Charles II stayed in the house in 1650 during his first attempt to wrest back his crown; but it was during this stay that the Marquis of Argyll sealed his own fate by remonstrating with Charles over the bad company he kept, for ten years later his royal guest of Stirling had him thrown into the Tower of London and later beheaded for high treason.

Numerous other fragments from the past survive in the town,

glimpsed in wynds and closes which only Edinburgh can better. But the only other building to which I propose to turn is a piece of Victorian classicism on the Dumbarton road, a couple of hundred yards from the King's Knot, once perhaps part of a pleasaunce of James V. This building is the Smith Institute. Thomas Stuart Smith was one of those admirable nineteenth-century figures in Dundreary whiskers whom to-day we smile at as eccentric if not misguided, and whose aspirations we damn from the security of an age which believes that the State should supply all our wants. Mr. Smith spent his life in passionate devotion to painting, and scarcely set foot in the Stirling from which his family came, but his last visit there was devoted to arranging for the town to inherit his not inconsiderable fortune. Soon after, he died at Avignon, where his gift to Stirling is actually recorded on the headstone. The paintings which he bequeathed for the most part are not in the taste of to-day, or even yesterday, although they do include pictures by Fantin-Latour, Cox and Richard Parkes Bonington; but he also made provision for a museum, and among the medley of material which this contains is a great number of bygones, many of them local, which grow in interest with the years. The splendid Stirling Heads from the Castle, mentioned earlier, no doubt will always be the centrepiece, but there are weapons and furniture and domestic bric-à-brac which are essential complements to the historic old buildings of the town. My hope would be that the resurgence of Stirling as a university town may enable the Institute not merely to present these bygones as they should be presented, but to create a choice little gallery of painting and decorative art for the pleasure of citizens, students and visitors, which would delight the gentle, generous ghost of the late Mr. Smith.

Stirling is the centre of an interesting countryside, however discouraging the approach to it from the south may seem. It is, of course, astride the road to the north, as well as the route to the West Highlands; but those are territories outside the scope of this book. Yet for a few miles this north road passes through Lowland country, and the short stretch from Stirling to Bridge of Allan is worth lingering on.

On the eastern edge of Stirling itself is Cambuskenneth Abbey. A lofty tower or campanile is the only substantial fragment of the abbey which survives, and even this does not impress as well proportioned, but one must keep in mind the absence of church and other buildings.

At the top of the tower is a well-lit chamber in which it is probable the Scottish parliaments met from time to time, and Professor Hannah said it was tempting to think that Robert Bruce's Parliament of July, 1325, may have used it. Certainly the tower in the main appears to be of the fourteenth century. Portions of the ruins may be considerably earlier. This was one of David I's many ecclesiastical foundations. The English probably sacked the place more than once, but the present ruinous state dates from much later than the English invasion. In 1604 it came into possession of the Earl of Mar, who used it as a quarry for stones when he built Mar's Work in Stirling, described earlier, and in course of time it was further robbed for the building of stane dykes in the neighbourhood. But it was a royal abbey, and in 1864 the Society of Antiquaries of Scotland uncovered among the ruins the burial-place of James III and his queen, Margaret of Denmark. James died after the battle of Sauchieburn, near by, in 1488. The remains were reburied and a stone erected to the memory of the dead sovereigns by command of their descendant, Queen Victoria.

The north road at one time crossed the Old Brig, now closed to traffic. The bridge itself is worth an inspection. It is five and a half centuries old. But the bridge at which Wallace defeated the Earl of Surrey in 1297, when many of the English army were drowned in the Forth, has long since disappeared. A short distance further on, the road swings round by the Abbey Craig, upon which the Gothic monument to Wallace itself had achieved the century and become an accepted part of the landscape. The sword exhibited as Wallace's is a two-hander typical of the late fifteenth and sixteenth centuries, and the cautious visitor should recall that Wallace, as a knight of his time, would arm himself with the more manageable weapon known to collectors of arms as a 'knightly' sword. This sword had the distinction of being stolen in 1936 in one of those grand, vain gestures on behalf of Scottish freedom which are made at intervals, but on this particular occasion the symbol of revolt might have been selected with more discrimination. Now the wooded slopes of the policies of Airthrey Castle, north of the Craig, belong to the new University of Stirling and Bridge of Allan's pleasant main street will no doubt become an academic precinct.

The Carse of Stirling, the rich plain through which the Forth winds, is packed with history, as one expects of any such area in a country not abundantly supplied with productive land. Unlike most comfortable agricultural regions it also provided some spectacular prospects. The best time to reconnoitre it is in autumn or early spring, when the air is clear and sharp and the Perthshire peaks are snow-capped and even the shoulders of the Ochils may be white. Take the Balloch road out of Stirling. It leaves behind the crags of Stirling Castle to follow the north fringe of the Gargunnock and Fintry Hills and the Campsie Fells. The villages around here, Gargunnock and Kippen, are tucked away elusively in the shadow of the hills and scarcely see the sun in winter, although they have an ancient reputation as healthful spots. Kippen until recently was noted for its aged vine of such vast size that it yielded 2,000 bunches of grapes annually, but that is gone. With Arnprior and Buchlyvie we are really over the verge into the Highlands in that this is Buchanan clan country right up to the shores of Loch Lomond, although the Buchanan lands are now in the possession of the Duke of Montrose. Arnprior is astride a cross-roads. The south road climbs up to Fintry and into the Campsies, and can be recommended for the views which it commands. The north road winds down to the Forth, and through the Flanders Moss. I do not imagine that visitors in search of relics of the past or bits of history ever stop to look at the Moss, this wide tract of splendid farm-land as flat as a table and apparently without arresting feature. In fact, it is one of the most unusual historical monuments in the country, a memorial to the agricultural revolution in general and to one man in particular: a great judge and writer, Lord Kames. Just two hundred years ago Lord Kames came into possession of the estate of Blairdrummond, which embraced the neighbouring Moss within its territories. The Moss was then a huge bog laced with black pools, a blanket of quaking peat anything up to twelve feet thick, but under the peat lay good alluvial soil, and although the judge was then aged seventy he put his formidable mind to the problem of reclamation. Manual removal was out of the question: the labour cost would have been far beyond his means. But it occurred to him that if the excavated peat could be sluiced into the river by water-power his aim would be achieved far more cheaply. The whole story can be read in the *Statistical Account* of 1799. Channels were cut down into the clay and water driven through them. The man-power to dig and off-load the peat was re-cruited from the poor, workless Highlanders uprooted by the measures taken to repress the Highlands after Culloden, so that Lord Kames helped to solve a social as well as an economic problem. The 'moss-lairds', as these Highlanders were called, had a bad time of it for years as they were distrusted by the local farmers; but the judge, and after his death in 1782 at the age of eighty-six, his son George Drummond, guided the scheme with faith and skill and boundless energy, engineering roads, offering prizes for the amount of peat cut, introducing a great mill-wheel for water-power, and by 1817 the project begun in 1766 was achieved. Many a poor 'moss-laird' had become a rich farmer.

The rich soil of the Carse had been laid down as mud by the sea which, at the end of the Ice Age, covered this entire area as far west as the outlying shoulders of Ben Lomond. Even now the land is only about thirty feet above sea-level, although the nearest salt water is fifteen miles or so away. The underlying clay is full of shells, and many skeletons of whales and other sea beasts have been found. Glaciers coming down out of the glens brought quantities of gravel and clay into the plain, and the mounds left by moraines trapped water and formed lakes. This is the origin of the beautiful Lake of Menteith a few miles north of the Moss. Covering rather more than a square mile, the lake has three islands. The largest, Inchmahome, has the ruins of a priory built in the thirteenth century for the Austin canons. Parts of the nave and choir have survived of the church in which David II was married in 1362 to his second wife, Margaret, and there are several medieval tombs. As a small girl, Mary Queen of Scots stayed in the priory for nearly a year after the battle of Pinkie in 1547, and prior to her sailing for France, and she is said to have busied herself in the garden called Queen Mary's Bower. On Inchmahome too is the burial-place of R. B. Cunninghame-Graham, the author; that romantic figure whose enthusiasms ranged from Scots nationalism to the cause of the gauchos of the South American pampas.

The south-eastern prospect from Stirling seems to offer much less promise than the others. The same flattish carse-lands stretch away to a low line of hills, but they are dotted with shale-bings, the pencils of factory chimneys, and above all with clustering industrial townships. This is the edge of the coal-and-iron belt which girds the loins of Scotland. However, it would be wrong to think it not worth exploring.

Almost on the very edge of Stirling itself is the much-discussed site of the battle of all battles in Scottish history.

The prosaic sign 'Bannockburn' confronts the motorist entering a little mining town a mile or two along the Edinburgh road. No sentimental sighs need be drawn here, and no housing scheme eccentricities need outrage patriotic feelings, for the village of Bannockburn did not exist until long centuries after the battle of that name had been fought. The place of the battle is a little to the west of the village, accessible by the Stirling–Glasgow road. It, too, might have been covered by housing schemes or factories, but the ground, or fifty-eight acres of it, were bought by a national committee, and in 1932 handed over to the National Trust for Scotland. More recently the Trust has built a rotunda with panels commemorating the course of the battle, and in 1964, on the 650th anniversary, Her Majesty the Queen unveiled the great equestrian statue of the Bruce carried out by Mr. C. d'O. Pilkington Jackson. There are many books on the battle, but the Trust offers a succinct, authoritative account by General Sir Philip Christison, latest and most professional of many students of a contest which emotion and the mists of time have tended to distort.

From the Scots angle at least, the focal point of this historic landscape is the Borestone, fragments of which are built into a pedestal. By repute, the Borestone is the socket in which the shaft of Bruce's standard was set. Bruce was a shrewd general and placed his troops well, on a height flanked by the Bannock Burn, a less negotiable stream then than now, especially in its lower reaches in front of the Scots' position where it was partly tidal and set among bogs. The English army had not the enormous strength which tradition gave it, but it counted about 20,000 men against Bruce's army of not much more than 5,000 and morale among the English remained high, as well it might, until the first day of the battle (23rd June). The English army must have been a magnificent sight as it moved relentlessly to the relief of the garrison at Stirling, the summer heat shimmering and the sun flashing on pennon and polished helm. But on this 23rd rash de Bohun lost his life to Bruce himself at the cost of the royal battleaxe, and Randolph Moray showed that resolute pikemen could throw back a charge of heavy armoured knights; so that when a bright dawn lit up the field on the 24th Edward's host watched the Scots at their prayers with a sense of fore-

boding, although the King did not share it. The English van, under
Gloucester, swept in to the attack, but again the Scottish pikemen in
their schiltrons set up a hedge of spears, and Gloucester himself was
among the knights slain. Increased by riderless horses, confusion seized
the main body of the English army. With bog-land behind and on the
flanks the English could turn neither this way nor that and were compressed by the slow, grim advance of the Scottish pikes. Bowmen soon
to be dreaded at Creçy and Agincourt poured their shafts into the flank
of the Scots, but Bruce made instant use of his small force of light
cavalry under Sir Alexander Keith to disperse the archers, and the
deadly compression of the English army went on. At last Bruce saw the
climax. He ordered Macdonald of the Isles to go in with his clansmen,
and the English line began to crack. The English leaders saw their
failure and prevailed on Edward to flee before it was too late. With his
bodyguard he left the field. Not only his own men saw his retreating
standard, but so did a force of about 2,000 Scots which had been concealed behind what has come to be called the Gillies' Hill, and this
force came pouring down towards the battle to turn defeat into rout.
This is an incident dear to the history books, which used gleefully to
describe the 2,000 as mere camp-followers, or in the case of the late
Tom Johnson's *History of the Working Classes in Scotland* as a sort of
proletarian Nemesis; but General Christison puts the matter into per-
spective, making it clear they were the 'small folk'—crofters, artisans
and the like—whom Bruce had kept as a hidden reserve, probably for
just some such purpose as they did in fact serve. The routed English
forces piled into the gully of the Bannock, filling it with horses and
men, and died by the hundred lower down in the tidal waters of the
Forth itself. Standing on this knoll by the Borestone, one suddenly
loses all sight of the council housing schemes and the chimneys and the
shale bings, for the main factors in that momentous battle are there as
clear as on that summer day in 1314: the encircling burn itself, the
Gillies' Hill, Coxet Hill and, away beyond, the Forth which trapped
the retreat and the rock of Stirling Castle which was Edward II's
objective. The sculptor might well have chosen to devise a 'significant'
Bruce, a monument with a smooth hole or two for the wind to sigh
through; but instead he modelled the features on the crags of the dead
king's skull and took counsel with students of armour on his trappings

of war. I think myself that the authenticity of this heroic bronze must have more to say in this place than would some wholly subjective whimsy, however eloquent that might have been for a few.

Stirling is close to the western end of the Ochils and to the Vale of the Devon, to give it what is perhaps an older name. One of many faults of the motor-car as an aid to exploration is that it tempts people to go too far too quickly, and strangers feeling they have Oban or even John o' Groats within their reach would not wander into a road through the Ochil hillfoot villages and towns. Even to-day there is an air of rural seclusion about the Devon valley. Mineral wealth underlying all this part of the country does make itself apparent here and there but, as in the Border country, there is a tradition of textile manufacture based on the product of the local sheep, and this has sufficiently determined the pace of development to give the region a sort of bloom of contentment in sharp contrast to the industrialised lower part of the Carse not so many miles away. The burns tumbling off the Ochil slopes towards the Devon have their woollen mills, but they are not spoilt by them. Townships have grown up where the little glens come down to the river. What they hold is not of great note, historically speaking, but some of them are pretty places. Blair Logie and Menstrie are good examples. Alva, again, is a manufacturing town, but with numerous amenities. For a time it had some repute for its silver mine, and there is still a Silver Glen. The mine was rich enough to free its owner, Sir John Erskine, from the sentence of outlawry passed upon him for his part in the 'Fifteen, and the ore from it was assayed by no less an authority than Sir Isaac Newton. Tillicoultry is another of the hillfoot mill-towns. Its serges had fame as far back as the sixteenth century. From Tillicoultry to Dollar is perhaps the finest stretch of this road by the Devon. Dollar itself is a well-built town with an air of greater sophistication than its neighbours, and is celebrated for its academy; but its comfortable modern look belies a long and troubled history, whether or no there is truth in the derivation of the town's name from the word 'dolour'. Castle Gloom, indeed, was the name of Castle Campbell, close to the town, until 1489; but it may be 'Dollar' comes from the Gaelic for a dark place and derives from the hanging woods in the glen. The Campbells, kinsmen of the Argyll family, owned much of the land around Dollar from the fifteenth century. The

Argyll zeal for the Reformers brought John Knox to the castle for a brief visit, and while there he is said to have 'taught certane dayes'. Montrose's men burned the castle in 1644. Its grim feudality endures, for it is built on to, and into, the rock itself, with dungeon beneath. As in the case of Stirling, there is a sixteenth-century palace block, with glorious views to the south. The castle and the approach to it on its crag between the Water of Sorrow and the Water of Care are spectacular.

Some miles above Dollar the Devon breaks back sharply to the north-west at Crook of Devon, coming down through Glen Devon from its source high in the hills. Below the Crook is some of the most dramatic scenery in the course of this short river, which falls about 2,000 feet in thirty miles. Rumbling Bridge, the Devil's Mill and the Cauldron Linn succeed one another. Scenery in itself is not one of the prime concerns of this book, but I cannot resist one quote from an early guidebook as a commentary on these places. 'Rumbling Bridge', we are told, 'is so named from the hollow brawling of the water while forcing its way among large fragments of impending rock; and as it hurries along boiling and foaming in wildest tumult the whole scenery adjacent is characteristic of that fantastic rudeness which Nature delights in exhibiting amid the roar of cascades and the thunder of cataracts.' Victorian verbiage is unfashionable to-day, but sometimes its profusion can outdo the achievements of photography. Yet Robert Burns is reputed to have turned away from the Rumbling Bridge without comment!

three

St. Andrews
and the Kingdom of Fife

St. Andrews should be the climax, not the starting-point, of an exploration of Fife. Unless one descends upon it from the sea, like the Vikings
or like the French at the time of the Reformation, it is the end not the
beginning of a countryside and has nothing between it and the coast of
Norway. From the Pilgrims' View on the road from Crail it has the
dreamlike quality of so many ancient university towns, but it is unique
in that its spires break the long, sweeping curve of the surf on a glorious
beach bordering the misted green sward of the most celebrated golf-
course in the world.

On closer acquaintance its attractions increase. It has always been
curiously isolated. Even in modern times access to it by rail involves
changing from a main-line train at Leuchars into a short string of local
coaches plying the few miles to the town, coaches which have borne
to and from the terminus not merely distinguished academics in plenty
from every continent but also probably every golfer of repute in the
history of the game. Unlike so many modern meccas, St. Andrews must
disappoint few of the pilgrims who flock there. It has everything they
look for. To the well-tended monuments of past centuries is added an
aura of present good living, in bookshop window, in glimpse of ancient
lawn, in the whiff of cigar smoke in a hoary wynd or vennel, and the
ancient stones are warmed to life by the red gowns of pretty under-
graduettes, their shadows livened by the white wings of gulls calling
from the crowsteps.

The town's importance in Scottish affairs stems from its ecclesiastical prominence. Its association with the relics of St. Andrew is, of course, there in the background but very early it became a Culdee settlement and by about 900 it took over the primacy from Abernethy and grew into the Canterbury of Scotland. The Cathedral, now ruinous, at one time was the largest in Scotland, and it is still possible to appreciate its scale although so much of the fabric has been robbed to provide material for houses and fortifications for the townsmen. Building began around 1160 and the remains show various phases of Norman work, but the Cathedral was not consecrated until 1318, when the ceremony took place in the presence of Robert the Bruce. Its ruins symbolise a troubled history, for, as we have seen in the previous chapter, Edward I robbed the nave of its lead for his siege-engines in 1304; in 1409 a

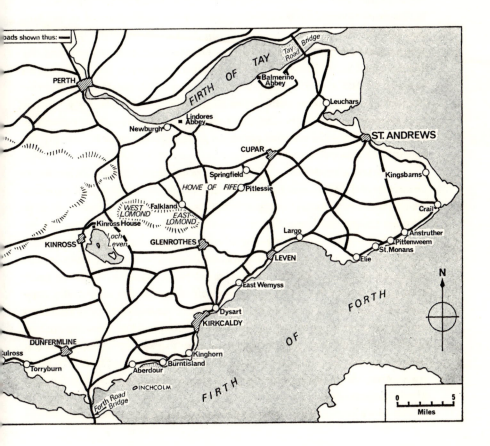

storm brought down the gable of the south transept, and at the Reformation there was a four-day 'cleaning of the temple' which resulted in the wholesale destruction of 'images'. One almost certain victim of the mob's zeal is the beautiful head of a bishop in the cathedral museum. Its features have been damaged, probably deliberately, but the planes of the face are moulded with some of the power of Egyptian royal sculpture and the mitre shows exquisite decorative detail. There are indeed a number of fine things in the little museum, some of them Celtic work, some medieval, some post-Reformation. The most remarkable is a portion of a carved stone sarcophagus of the ninth century, dug up in the vicinity. This ranks as one of the most important pieces of its period in Scotland. Its main panel depicts a hunting scene with exotic animals such as lions and apes, and the end panels show Celtic and Norse motifs similar to those of contemporary manuscripts and metalwork. A rare medieval object in the museum is a carved effigy of a master-mason, one of only two to have survived north of the Border. But St. Andrews has several ancient churches. In some respects more interesting than the Cathedral is the nearby church of St. Rule or St. Regulus. Its tower is one of the landmarks of the town, rising to 108 feet. It dates from the twelfth century and belonged to the Augustinian priory. Bishop Robert completed it, one of six canons brought by Alexander I from Nostell to found a priory at Scone, and on the evidence of the *Scotichronicon* the Bishop, who died in 1159, is buried in the church. Legend has it that St. Rule brought the relics of St. Andrew from Patras, in Achaia, in the fourth century and that he was shipwrecked here, and that he received the gift of a district called the Boar's Chase, so named because it comprised several parishes through which a notoriously savage boar was hunted and eventually killed. Then again, in Northgate is the church of St. Salvator, founded in 1450 by Bishop Kennedy with the college of the same name. Kennedy's arms are carved above the entrance, less easy to remove by the Reformation mob than the 'images' which no doubt occupied the flanking niches. Like other bishops of St. Andrews, Kennedy wielded great power in Scotland, was adviser to two kings and regent to a third. His arms appear on a fine, late Gothic ogival arch in the outer wall. The tomb of the Bishop has been sadly mutilated, but even so there is nothing else in Scotland quite like it. A French craftsman probably wrought it.

Close to the harbour and the sea, the Cathedral and its precincts form the focal point of the town. From it fan out eastwards the three principal streets, Southgate, Marketgate and Northgate, and shoreward of these Swallowgate leads to The Scores. People tend to draw comparisons between St. Andrews on the one hand and Oxford and Cambridge, but the points of similarity are far outweighed by the differences, for St. Andrews is one of the most typical of old Scottish towns. Its real quality lies in the domestic buildings dating from the sixteenth to the early eighteenth century scattered along the first three streets I have mentioned and in the linking lanes and wynds. They are plain, sedate houses, with no ornament except perhaps above the door-lintel, yet their way of projecting into or retiring beyond the street building-line lends individuality which grows on closer acquaintance. Occasionally, there is a delightful outside stair, or a corbelled feature. On the roofs, pantiles are not uncommon. Interiors are equally pleasing, often with moulded fireplaces and sometimes with ceiling-beams of Baltic timber, and one or two still have their sixteenth-century painted ceilings. Of the larger houses perhaps the finest is the one known as Queen Mary's House, now the St. Leonard's School library, close to the Cathedral at the east end of Southgate. It is believed to have been built by a merchant called Scrymgeour in 1523, but has been added to at various times. In the west wing there is a panelled room associated with Mary Queen of Scots.

The spiritual and intellectual importance of St. Andrews always outweighed all else, and it was never a seat of government nor of military significance. Even its ancient castle was the episcopal palace, and the Fore Tower of this is probably a surviving portion of the original structure built by Bishop Roger in 1200. It is now almost completely in ruins. The ruins, however, are extensive and picturesque and are peopled by the ghosts of great figures of the Reformation times. Indeed this fortress symbolises the spirit which the Reformers sought to destroy. As early as 1433 the Bohemian Hussite, Paul Craw, was burnt in St. Andrews. Patrick Hamilton, disciple of Luther, followed him to the stake here in 1528. Man after man who learned in the schools of the Continent to doubt the rule of Rome met his end here in the East Neuk of Fife. Cardinal David Beaton pursued heresy without mercy from this strong palace on the sea's edge. His ultimate weapon was the stake, but in the floor of the prison in the Sea Tower one may still inspect the 'bottle-dungeon', a pit with overhanging roof dug out of the rock, into the foul dark of which the Cardinal threw many a reformer. The Cardinal was a focus of Catholicism even for English enemies of his Church, and Henry VIII plotted his removal. Whether George Wishart was implicated in such a plot may never be known—it would be nothing to his discredit in that bitter time—but for his faith, if for no other reason, he became the last of the St. Andrews martyrs, and from his window close by, Beaton watched the flames consume him. Buchanan tells that before he was strangled Wishart foretold the oppressor's death. Less than three months later, on 5th May 1546, early in the morning, a band of men forced their way into the Cardinal's chamber, cut him down despite his plea of being a priest, and threw the body into the bottle-dungeon with a quantity of salt 'to keep him from stinking' until 'his brethren the Bishops' should dispose of him, to quote from John Knox's own words. The deed enraged town and countryside, and the band of assassins shut themselves in the castle.

Although the loon was weill away
The deed was foully done.

In the castle they were joined by others of their mind, including Knox himself. The following year a French fleet took the castle. Knox and some of his companions were consigned to the galleys at Nantes. A remarkable survival from the siege of 1546 is a mine driven by the besiegers to get under the Fore Tower and a countermine by the besieged which apparently foiled the attempt.

There were three colleges in the University of St. Andrews, which is the most ancient of the Scottish universities. The oldest is St. Salvator's. It came into being about 190 years later than the oldest of the Oxford foundations, Merton and Balliol, which preceded Peterhouse at Cambridge by about twenty years. Of all four colleges, only Merton and St. Salvator's possess their ancient chapel buildings, though unhappily the St. Andrews chapel has been considerably restored. Relics in the possession of which the Scottish university is unrivalled, however, are the silver maces or verges which anyone interested in medieval craftsmanship should make a point of seeing. The mace of St. Salvator's is the least old, but an inscription above the fleuron dates it eleven years after

6   *St Andrews Cathedral*

the founding of the college and gives the name of the maker, John Maiel, who was warden of the Paris Incorporation of Goldsmiths at this time. The oldest mace, that of the Faculty of Arts, is also French. Records indicate its date as between 1414 and 1418. The third mace, that of the Faculty of Canon Law, is modelled on the Arts mace but is almost certainly a Scottish piece of the same half of the century. All are in Gothic style and, with the Glasgow University mace, are the oldest pieces of their kind in Britain. Their ecclesiastical form reflects the fact that churchmen invariably presided over university affairs before the Reformation.

To most eyes the most pleasing of the colleges is St. Mary's which, with the University Library, is in Southgate. A great deal of reconstruction of the building took place early last century, but the sixteenth-century Founder's Tower and many other features are intact. To come in from the street and be faced with wide lawns and trees and creeper-covered walls is in this case certainly to be reminded of some Oxford quads. Archbishop James Beaton began by founding the college in 1537, and Archbishop Hamilton completed it sixteen years later. Now it houses the Faculty of Theology. In the garden is a fine sundial of 1664 and a thorn-tree reputedly planted by Mary Queen of Scots. The Library has many treasures, including the Bassandyne Bible and a copy of the Solemn League and Covenant, and among the college plate is the St. Mary's mazer, one of the small group of Scottish standing mazer bowls, a severely plain piece by Alexander Auchinleck, the Edinburgh goldsmith, which can be dated to about 1561, although a date inscribed on it is later by six years. The University also possesses the St. Leonard's mazer. It is entirely of silver—perhaps because the wooden bowl has been replaced—and is unmarked, but may be the one referred to in the St. Leonard's College Inventory of the Chamber for 1544. The church belongs to the University; but Hall and residences, some of which may be late sixteenth-century, are now part of St. Leonard's School for girls. The two colleges of St. Leonard and St. Salvator were united in 1747.

In these times of highly professionalised sport Scotland no longer preserves her old domination of the national game of golf. Nevertheless, the Royal and Ancient Golf Club of St. Andrews remains the world's leading club and dictates the laws of the game wherever it be played,

7 *Leuchars Church, Fife*

from China to Peru. The four great courses are laid out here on perfect, natural turf, and hazards of the Old Course famous (or notorious) everywhere, such as Hell Bunker or the Swilcan Burn, are contrived from natural hazards which through time have become features of the game. That last green on which so many reputations have been made or lost, far from being a preserve of members, is overlooked by the windows of the town to which the course belongs. The race of true professionals, craftsmen who made the implements and taught the game, is gone, replaced by sleek specialists, just as the expressive old Scots names for the clubs—baffie, mashie, niblick, cleek—have been replaced by meaningless serial numbers, and Tom Morris and Allan Robertson and Andra' Auchterlonie no longer look out with their critical eyes from their shops on the edge of the green. Unlike the courses, the Royal and Ancient clubhouse itself is an exclusive place. It is also a treasure-house of the history of the game. The club goes back to 1754, and the silver trophy club first played for in May of that year is still preserved, with its collection of silver balls—and one gold one— presented by successive captains. Here, too, of course, are numerous clubs of past ages, among them a cleek of 1760, and balls which include a feather-ball made by Tom Morris and the first 'gutty' introduced about 1860. Portraits of captains on the walls include many famous figures, among them one painted by General Eisenhower.

St. Andrews has only one shortcoming for our present purpose, in that it is not centrally placed for making small excursions into the length and breadth of Fife. I propose to cover the county—and part of Kinross—by making two long journeys. The first is an exploration of the northern and central parishes.

Leuchars is the first stopping-place. From the exposed and sometimes rather draughty station platform it looks an unpromising spot, its main feature an R.A.F. station; but investigation will disclose one of the two finest small Norman churches in the country. Chancel and apse of this parish church are all that remains of a building erected around 1185, dedicated in 1244. It is the exterior which is especially fine, with shafted arcading round the walls in two courses, the arches intersecting on the lower. Marks of the axes used to dress the stones eight centuries ago may be recognised without much difficulty. The lantern tower added in the seventeenth century is something of an oddity. In that same century the church was the scene of an incident significant in Scottish history, yet not so well known. In 1618 Alexander Henderson was presented to the charge of Leuchars by the Archbishop of St. Andrews, but when he arrived he found the doors of the church bolted by the men of the parish and had to climb in through a window. Years later, his Presbyterian successor in the charge recalled the incident by preaching a sermon on the text: *Verily, verily I say unto you, He that entereth not by the door into the sheepfold, but climbeth up some other way, the same is a thief and a robber*. Henderson, so far from resenting this, in 1638 publicly confessed his error in thus forcing himself on his flock, and became not only one of the great leaders of the Covenanters but the author of the Covenant itself.

It is only a few miles from Leuchars to Balmerino on the shores of the Tay, facing across shoal waters to the Carse of Gowrie. Not a great deal of the Abbey of Balmerino has survived the attack by an English fleet which came up the Tay in 1547, the commander of which recorded shamelessly that on Christmas night of that year he had a skirmish with some Scots at 'Balmuryno', killed four horsemen and 'burned the Abbey and everything in it'. The church and cloister of this Cistercian house, founded in 1226, have little to show now but foundations and the stumps of walls, but the sixteenth-century chapter-house is complete enough to indicate something of the beauty that is lost. After Balmerino, the road westwards is uneventful enough for a matter of ten miles, always with the compensation of views across the Firth to the Sidlaws and beyond, until it passes another ruinous twelfth-century abbey, Lindores. There is not a great deal left to delight an untrained eye either here or at Balmerino, but it is worth pausing at these abbey sites if only because they are such good examples of that feeling for potentially good agricultural land which the medieval orders showed in Scotland, as elsewhere. They were bold missionaries; but coming from the fertile valleys of France to the Yorkshire dales, then the Borders and on into the north, always they had the wisdom to found their houses where the harvest of the soil would help the harvest of the spirit. Even now the orchards of neighbouring Newburgh are excellent, but it seems to have been the Benedictines of Lindores who introduced the pear-tree to these parts. Before that, Celtic communities of monks had also worked the land here, but they had no system of lay-brethren to care for secular affairs and were quite unable to exploit the rich potentialities of the countryside.

At Newburgh the spurs of the Ochils reach out to the Tay. If we skirt the hills and move south, Loch Leven comes into view, lying in the flat lands between the Ochils and the Cleish Hills and the Lomonds of Fife. Loch Leven is in Kinross not Fife, but until 1485 Fife and Kinross were one and it is convenient to link them. The county town, Kinross, is close to the loch. It is, I should think, a pleasant town to live in, but historically it is not noteworthy. Its most remarkable feature is Kinross House, the gates of which are close to the main street. For many connoisseurs of architecture, Kinross House is the most beautiful mansion in Scotland. Not long after its erection, about 1685, it is described by Sir Robert Sibbald as a house 'which for situation, contrivances, prospects, avenues, courts, gravel-walks and terraces, and all hortulane ornaments, parks and planting, is surpassed by few in this country'. There was a long period of neglect, when the place was unoccupied, but its former glories have been restored for the past couple of generations, and its gardens are among the best formal gardens in the north. Sir William Bruce of Balcaskie, architect to the King, built the house for his own use, although it is said to have been intended for the Duke of York had the proposed Exclusion Bill prevented his becoming James II. Scandal has whispered that the estate was purchased and the house built on the proceeds of Bruce's office as Clerk of the Bills, and the receipt of moneys taken from fined Covenanters, but the architect had a prosperous enough practice and his commissions had included the rebuilding of the Palace of Holyroodhouse. Kinross House is an elegant essay in late seventeenth-century Renaissance style, exquisite in its detail. The exterior is four-square and perhaps just a little severe, but the interior is delightful, with an entrance-hall and staircase of great beauty, the stair with a baroque oak balustrade of a richness unusual in Scotland, and there is a magnificent salon with a coved ceiling splendidly decorated. Bruce's crest and his monogram, incorporating a wife's initials, appear in more places than one.

Loch Leven from the terrace of Kinross House is a lovely stretch of water; from other aspects it is not one of Scotland's choicer lochs, except in the eye of the angler, for whom it means a pink-fleshed variety of trout with special virtues both as a sporting fish and as an item on the menu. The loch is associated in most minds with the imprisonment and escape of Mary Queen of Scots in 1567–8, that romantic last adventure which preluded defeat and the lingering years of confinement at Fotheringhay. One wonders how many 'anglers' have trawled the oozy bottom in vain for the keys thrown overboard by young William Douglas! The Castle had in fact a long history before Mary saw it. The ubiquitous Edward I laid siege to it in 1301, and an English army in Edward III's time tried to reduce the garrison by damming the River Leven and raising the level of the loch. Nor was Mary the first State prisoner, for Archibald, Earl of Douglas was committed to Loch Leven Castle by James I in 1429. But one might even say that Castle Island itself has less significance in Scottish history than St. Cerf's Island, a mile away over the loch. There was a Culdee priory here, reputedly established by St. Serf after he received the island from the Pictish king, Brude, in the seventh century. David I converted the Culdee community into canons regular, a prior of whom in the fifteenth century was Andrew of Wyntoun, whose *Orygynale Cronykil of Scotland*, written doubtless on the island, is in its later portions an invaluable source of Scottish history.

Beyond the Lomonds, in a sheltered hollow, lies Falkland. There have been settlements here since very early times. There are forts on several points of high ground, a strong one on the summit of the East Lomond itself. The occupants of this last may have been people of considerable culture, because among the things they left is a carving of a bull incised on sandstone reminiscent of the Burghead bulls, a relic now in the National Museum of Antiquities in Edinburgh. The medieval settlement lay in the hollow. Here, on a hillock, was the Tower of Falkland, destroyed by the English in 1337 and presumably rebuilt, since Albany is said to have starved his nephew, the Duke of Rothesay, to death here, in 1402, as *The Fair Maid of Perth* relates. In the fifteenth century the Castle became the property of the Crown by forfeiture, and about 1500 the Palace of Falkland was built by James IV and improved upon by James V. Cromwell's troops destroyed a wing of the Palace, but the south wing is intact. Like Stirling Palace, it reflects a Renaissance spirit. Indeed Falkland, Stirling, Linlithgow and Holyroodhouse in Edinburgh are the four great examples of what has been called the 'Court School' of building, a school which completely turns away from the vertical, fortified 'keep' tradition to a style able to reflect social status both in structure and embellishment. So by contrast with the many grim medieval castles, Falkland's south wing is Italianate, with columns and sculptured heads of sovereigns—the 'five grate stane imagis' which are recorded, which Dr. Richardson considers the equal of anything done in the France of Francis I, and two figures carved by one Peter Flemisman. Clearly Falkland was designed to bring some light and laughter into the lives of James V's two successive wives from the gay Court of France. There were painted ceilings and, no doubt, rich furnishings, there was hunting to be had in the hills around and hawking too—Falkland may well be 'falcon land'—and there was even a caichpule or tennis-court in the Palace, now restored and the only surviving real tennis-court in Scotland, happily again in use. But for all King James's gay purpose, it was at Falkland that he died after his defeat at Solway Moss, and it was to the wall of one of its rooms that he turned away his head when he heard of the birth of his daughter, to be Mary Queen of Scots, saying sadly; 'It cam wi' a lass, and it'll gang wi' a lass'.

The country between Falkland and the town of Cupar to the east is the penultimate battle-ground in the struggle leading to the establishment of Protestantism in 1560. Mary of Guise, second of the two brides for whom James V had embellished the Palace, had her base at Falkland with an army of French troops and troops in France's pay. She seemed to have barred the escape of Knox and his Reformers and the few fighting men with them. Despite a threat from the Archbishop of St. Andrews that he would be greeted by culverins if he preached, Knox mounted the pulpit and thundered his challenge based on the text of the money-changers in the temple. It was a call to arms. From all Fife and the counties around armed men rallied. The French commander signed a truce. The Reformers dispersed. The French took advantage of this, and for a time seemed to hold the advantage, so that Mary of Guise triumphantly demanded: 'Where is John Knox his God?—My God is stronger than his, even in Fife!' But again the Reformers gathered and drove Mary back out of Fife and into Lothian, and in the Castle of Edinburgh she died.

The Howe of Fife and the country to the east of it is, for me, the heart of Fife. There are no great mansions or castles or battlefields in it, but when the corn is yellow and the sun beats on the pantiled roofs and makes blue shade under the beeches, there is bucolic charm here that is rare in the north. It inspired one great Scottish painter of modern times, Leslie Hunter; it bred another of long ago, Sir David Wilkie, who was born at Cults and took as the subject of his first picture Pitlessie Fair. There are pretty, sleepy villages such as Dairsie, with its sixteenth-century bridge, and Springfield, and Ceres, with the so-appropriate name. The market-town is Cupar, but the atmosphere of the surrounding country pervades this too. The parish churches both of Cupar and of Ceres are well worth visiting. St. Michael's at Cupar has been much rebuilt, but has a beautiful Renaissance spire of 1620, built at the minister's own expense, and a fine fifteenth-century tomb with a knightly effigy of one of the Fernie family. Such knightly tombs are rare in Scotland, but there is another in an almost perfect state in Ceres church.

Mile for mile, the south coastal road of Fife has more of architectural and historical interest than is packed into any similar stretch of road in Scotland. Indeed there is so much that it is possible here only to take samples. It is worth allotting two or three days to this journey of a mere seventy miles.

The road strikes inland a little as it leaves St. Andrews and goes by way of Kingsbarns to Crail. It was at Crail on 3rd June, 1559, that Knox proclaimed he would preach the following Sunday at St. Andrews —a challenge thrown in the teeth of the Archbishop himself. The parish kirk where he preached is simple and lovely, much of it twelfth or thirteenth century, including one of those squat towers with small, conical steeples of later date which are rather typical of Fife. The ordinary dwelling-houses of the village are many of them seventeenth century, seven or eight of those in the High Street carrying their dates above the door or elsewhere. Vernacular houses of this sort, usually modest in scale, are the real glory of the Fife coast villages and towns. Theirs is a living style, accommodating itself to the rocky coast, clustering around the little harbours, hoary with age yet delightfully capable of adaptation to modern times without loss of character, as more and more discriminating people are discovering. The Anstruthers are rich in them; so are Pittenweem and St. Monans. St. Monans possesses one of the best of the little towered kirks. 'Founded anew' by David II in the fourteenth century, the church is mostly of this period, and it is a real fishermen's church, washed by the sprays of south-easterly gales. Largo and Dysart are larger places, yet here again there are outcrops of those wrinkled walls and roofs which seem to grow out of the ground, Largo with its twisting, steep streets climbing from a sheltered harbour. Small as they are, these places bred some big names in the story of the sea. The statue of Robinson Crusoe in Largo commemorates Alexander Selkirk, the Largo man whose adventures Defoe probably heard about when travelling in Fife. Largo also produced Sir Philip Wood, admiral to James III and James IV, who flew his flag in the *Great St. Michael* and who is said to have cut a canal from his house to the kirk so that he could be rowed there in an eight-oar barge on Sundays!

One may become so preoccupied with the ordinary houses of the Fife coast that other interests are forgotten. Further inland, for example, there are fine mansions such as Kellie Castle, near St. Monans, a stately essay in the vernacular restored by Sir Robert Lorimer, and Balcarres, home of the Earl of Crawford, with its collection of superb works of art, although it should be said that such houses are not normally open for visitors. There are many prehistoric sites. The tumulus at Norrie's Law, near Largo, in 1819 produced a hoard of silverwork in or near a stone coffin. This hoard, now in the National Museum of Antiquities, includes curious Pictish ornaments some of which seem to have pagan, some Christian significance. Then again the shore has a number of caves with early associations. Jonathan's Cave at Wemyss has markings similar to those on certain Pictish sculptured stones, one of these the beautifully incised outline of an animal. A cave at Dysart associated with St. Serf points the origin of the village's name, as a 'desert' in the Celtic Church was a place of retreat.

Kirkcaldy is a prosperous town, considerably industrialised, but here too there are many old dwellings, some of which have been renovated. Among ancient buildings the most important is Ravenscraig Castle, set on a precipitous rock commanding the bay. It was built for Mary of Gueldres, queen to James II, in 1460, and she came here as a widow; but perhaps its most interesting feature, as Mr. Stewart Cruden explains, is that the gun-ports commanding the landward approach may be the first Scottish example of preconceived cannon-defences. In Mr. Cruden's words, 'it stands alone as an artillery fort among the many

castellated structures of the troubled fifteenth century'; and James, who had a deep interest in guns, was himself killed by the bursting of a cannon at Roxburgh while Ravenscraig was in process of building. Indeed Ravenscraig, a tower at Dysart, the isle of Inchkeith and the defences of Leith were to be envisaged as a chain of strong-points protecting the Forth against hostile men-of-war. They were never greatly tested; but three centuries later, when during the American War of Independence John Paul Jones and his squadron threatened the Forth towns, the Rev. Robert Shirra of Kirkcaldy used other methods to defeat the menace. With the American ships in sight, the Rev. Shirra knelt on the wet sands and prayed, and at once the wind veered into the west and blew the privateers back to the open sea. Numerous relics of Kircaldy's past are to be found in the town's museum, and under the same roof is one of the most pleasing little art galleries in the kingdom, notable for its collection of modern Scottish paintings bequeathed by a generous connoisseur who lived in the town.

Kinghorn, Burntisland and Aberdour are all worth lingering in. Burntisland's parish church is important as almost the only work of its kind erected in Scotland in the years following the Reformation. Built in 1592, it is unusual in being virtually square. It contains some quaint seventeenth and eighteenth-century painted panels and a curious, canopied magistrates' pew. In Aberdour, St. Fillan's church is an attractive Romanesque piece, with modifications of later dates. The Castle is ruinous but worth a visit. Aberdour is also the point from which a crossing may be made to the island of Inchcolm. Inchcolm Abbey from some aspects is as important a monument as Iona itself, because the fact of its being on an island has preserved it from casual despoilment, and the entire layout of this Augustinian foundation is there, although it must be said that a great deal of rebuilding went on in later times. Much of the first church dates from the twelfth century. In the south wall of the thirteenth-century choir is a fragment of mural painting, the most remarkable piece of medieval painting in Scotland. Probably it represents a funeral procession, and on stylistic grounds seems not later than the twelfth or thirteenth century. To the west of the main buildings is a small vault, the door of which, with its inward-sloping jambs, has a Celtic look, and some have held that this is the cell in which in 1123 a hermit of the early Church entertained Alexander I

Culross: the Market Cross

on a meagre fare of shellfish and milk. The King, who had barely escaped shipwreck, vowed to build a monastery on the island, and this is how the foundation came about. It became a well-endowed house, with many grants of land on the mainland, including the lands of Doni-bristle, and the name of Mortimer's Deep, given to the channel sep-arating the island from the Fife shore, is said to commemorate a land-owner of Aberdour whose body in its stone coffin was lost when being shipped for burial to the Abbey to which he had bequeathed his possessions.

Dunfermline, in the county second in size only to Kirkcaldy, is a natural centre for exploring West Fife. It has not the same heritage of charming old dwelling-houses as the coastal towns and villages possess, and at first sight is a rather plain commercial town, so that the ballad of Sir Patrick Spens, which tells of the King 'drinking the bluid-red wine' there, seems a little inappropriate; but the ballad is by no means entirely inappropriate, for 'Dunfermling toun' has seen a long succes-sion of kings, from Robert the Bruce who is buried there to Charles I who was born there. The material embodiment of Dunfermline's his-tory is its Abbey. This is one of the noblest groups of ecclesiastical remains in Scotland. The first church here was founded by Malcom Can-more and his queen, Margaret, towards the end of the eleventh cen-tury, and the foundations of this were discovered in 1916, and can be seen through gratings in the floor of the existing church; but this, the great abbey church, itself began building only about half a century after the earlier one, and the nave is one of the finest Romanesque monu-ments in the kingdom. The glory of it now lies mainly in its splendid columns, some with chevron or spiral ornament, and this so closely resembles similar ornament in Durham that it seems likely that the same masons were at work. The nave only survives, but some six-teenth-century additions are excellent Gothic work, merging well with the Norman. Malcolm and Margaret are buried in the precincts, and the tomb of King Robert is in the nave. His body was disinterred early in the nineteenth century, in wrappings of a material which may have been cloth-of-gold, and it was reburied. About five other early Scottish kings lie here, so that the Abbey has for Scotland some of the sig-nificance of Westminster for England. Indeed, in the thirteenth century the Pope granted to the Abbot and his successors the right to wear certain pontifical insignia, among them the mitre. The surrounding precincts are extensive and the conventual buildings impressive, the walls of the Palace dominating a sloping site above the Tower Burn—this probably the building which John Taylor, the Water-Poet, in 1618 describes as 'a delicate and princely mansion'. It became, certainly, a favourite home of James VI and Anne of Denmark, and this is how Charles I came to be born here. That Dunfermline could offer good fare and comfort in the Middle Ages is shown by prolonged though unwelcome visits by invading Kings of England. Edward I spent the winter of 1300 here, and four years later his queen also came. In later centuries the fortunes of the town were closely bound up with the growth and decline of the linen industry. Lint-mills were numerous in Fife, and the linens and damasks of Dunfermline were supremely fine—indeed still are, but economics and fashion have changed the demand. The magnificent park of Pittencrieff Glen, close to the Abbey, is a monument to Andrew Carnegie, who presented it to the town he was born in, and the great trusts which look after the funds, which the Pittsburgh millionaire left for educational purposes, are happily still administered from offices in his home town.

From Dunfermline it is a short return journey to the coast at Torryburn and Culross. This shore always gives me a sense of melancholy: perhaps because it is tucked away from the brisk breezes of the lower firth, perhaps because it is an ancient coal-mining district in decline. But it is particularly rich in old relics and associations, and Culross provides what is possibly the most perfect example extant of vernacular small-town building. It is now in the keeping of the National Trust for Scotland, in large part. Like so many of the villages we have just been considering, Culross is a royal burgh. This dignity was bestowed on it in 1588 by James VI, at a time when the coal and salt industries were bringing it prosperity. The King himself paid a visit to the coal-mine, the tunnels of which penetrated under the sea to a shaft on Preston Island, and when he emerged on the island to find water all about him the chronically suspicious monarch at once cried, 'Treason! Treason!' but his host, Sir George Bruce, allayed his fears and treated him to a magnificent feast in the Painted Chamber of his house in the Sandhaven. This house, known as The Palace, has been restored. The Painted Chamber is a good example of a type of interior decoration which the National Trust and H.M. Ministry of Public Building and Works have been trying to preserve, both here and elsewhere. An extraordinary monument to Sir George and his family is in the Abbey, on the hill above the town. Alabaster effigies of Sir George and his wife lie in a niche, with smaller effigies of his three sons and five daughters kneeling before the tomb. Obviously they are portraits, and as costume records they are also meticulously done. The monument is signed *John Mercer Fecit*, but it has been held that the figures are the work of Charles II's Master-Mason, Edmund Marshall (1578–1675). The Abbey is a Cistercian foundation dating from 1217. The Town House, like other buildings around the Forth, shows a marked Dutch influence and the tradition of the great *Rathaus* of the Low Countries can be discerned in its modest outlines. Dutch bells are common in the parish kirks of Fife and Lothian, and bulbous Dutch hanging-lamps, all reflecting the close relations of past centuries. The towers of the Abbey House at Culross show the same thing. But the greatest charm of Culross lies in its steep little streets and closes and gardens, with sudden glimpses of houses like The Study, with memories of a day when the haven was full of Dutch sails and the place echoed to the hammering of the girdle-makers, a trade in which Culross had such a monopoly that nearly every scone or oatcake baked in Scotland before 1715 must have owed its existence to a Culross girdle. A last lesson which can be learned from the little town is that these old Scots buildings should never be pulled down but adapted to changing needs, for the oil-heated con-servatories which are being sold as 'homes' to-day are pathetic alterna-tives to the snug and colourful 'little houses' of the Fife burghs.

four

Linlithgow
and West Lothian

Linlithgow is the third of the trio of towns in mid-Scotland which have more than their share in the making of history. The others are Stirling and Dunfermline. Not a great deal in quantity is left of Linlithgow's visible heritage, but the quality of what there is would be difficult to better anywhere in Scotland, and the replanning now under way should be contrived to focus attention on the Palace and St. Michael's Church. The setting is magnificent. The south entry, now effected by way of a brewery and a railway tunnel, could be modified to take full advantage of the downward plunge towards the sheltered main street and its neighbouring loch.

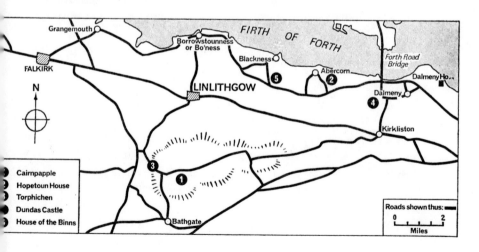

The Palace is quite the most remarkable thing of its kind in the country, and it is tragic it should have been left roofless after the King's troops set fire to it in 1746. It is built four-square around a central courtyard. Even in its present state it is a place of great dignity and power, ornamental enough in detail to recall past glories. Begun early in the fifteenth century, it went on building until 1539; and when the north quarter collapsed in 1607 it was rebuilt in Renaissance style. Dr. Douglas Simpson thinks that when Mary of Guise complimented her husband on this 'princely' palace she was using 'the language of courtesy', since she was familiar with the châteaux of the Loire. Perhaps he is right; but I should like to see the Palace reroofed and refurbished, gay hangings out and pennons flying, for with life returned to its gaunt visage and hollow eyes it might, in its gracious setting of hills and loch, challenge even the majesty of Blois. The sculptured detail is on altogether a more ambitious scale than is usual in Scotland, and the Royal Arms over the east entrance are massive and executed with great elegance. Inside the courtyard is, or has been, another large group of sculptures. Empty niches were once occupied by a figure of the Pope, and by a knight and a labouring man; but an Annunciation scene has survived, miraculously, and the quality of the Virgin and the Angel is of the first order. It is of course quite possible that French masons were employed on these sculptures, for the master-mason was a Frenchman, but a Scot called Ross seems to have been given the task of colouring the figures. The interior may well have matched its counterparts in France. I know of nothing along the Loire which one could with assurance say must have excelled the Lion Chalmer of Linlithgow. It is almost a hundred feet long and thirty-five feet from floor to ceiling, with a hammer-beam roof and a fireplace extending the full width of the room with moulded and carved mantel supported on massive columns. The records contain particulars of the royal plenishings which in the mind can instantly transform this great stone hall into a Court setting comparable with any in Europe, and although Scotland was a poor country the Stewarts were notoriously extravagant and proud. The Close or central courtyard is another feature of much grandeur. Four stair-towers occupy the angles, one of them the King's Turnpike, another probably the Queen's. The central fountain is now much damaged, but it has been a splendid piece, with sculptured pinnacles and heraldic beasts and flowers. It was fed by a spring outside the town, but on special occasions would run with the red wines of Bordeaux. King after Stewart king settled the Palace on his bride: James II on Mary of Gueldres, James III on Margaret of Denmark, James IV on Margaret Tudor, James V on Mary of Guise, and it was here that Mary Queen of Scots was born and spent her early years. Ironically, it may have been a Stewart who indirectly was the cause of the Palace's destruction, for the incendiarism of Hawley's dragoons in 1746 may not have been unconnected with the fact that the year before the Governor's wife had entertained the Prince there and was probably the last person to cause the fountain to run with wine.

Beside the gatehouse of the Palace is the Kirk of St. Michael. This is one of the most beautiful churches in Scotland, a fine piece of Gothic carried out with marked Scottish accent, such as the corbie-stepped gables of nave and aisles, the treatment of the porch, and the tower. The tower until early last century had a crown steeple, like St. Giles's in Edinburgh and King's College Chapel in Aberdeen, and this has been replaced recently with a metal structure in contemporary idiom which, to my mind, is out of place. The interior of the church is even finer than the exterior. It is simple, functional Gothic, with a wonderful complex of columns and groins. There is little sculpture. Probably some was lost at the Reformation, but there are four fine sandstone slabs which formed a retable for the altar and which depict scenes from the Passion. One at least dates from the fifteenth century, and any sculpture of this time in Scotland is precious. No notable monuments survive in the church, but St. Michael's must have had many royal worshippers. Certainly it was the scene of the apparition to James IV, the man in blue who pushed through the throng to warn James against the expedition to England which ended at Flodden. There was a belief that the Queen herself sent the man to dissuade her husband, and that he came and went by a concealed stair leading to the Palace next door. The incident is described by Scott in *Marmion*. The woodwork and furnishings of the church are modern, but on the pillars are carried some interesting and historic regimental colours, including those of the Scotch Brigade, a regiment raised in Linlithgowshire in 1793 and given the name of a more ancient body of the same name.

Although not a great many of the older houses have survived in the town, the main street preserves its medieval plan, up and down, now narrow, now wide. There are still a few sixteenth-century houses, and at that time the whole length of the High Street must have been flanked by harled or plastered dwellings with timber foreshots jutting over the street. It was from such a projecting housetop, now gone, that the Regent Moray was assassinated. His enemy, Hamilton of Bothwell-haugh, concealed himself behind the 'washing' hung on the balcony, and since this overhung a narrow part of the street it was an effective ambush. The Regent had been warned of trouble, but insisted on taking no precaution other than to ride at a smart canter, and Bothwellhaugh's shot was mortal. The assassin had a horse waiting for him in the garden behind the house, and escaped to the sea and to France.

There is much to see in the neighbourhood of Linlithgow, and the pity is that most of those who pass this way are in too much of a hurry to see it. One short visit which, for me, is more dramatic than the field of Bannockburn itself, is to the Antonine Wall. It is an industrial countryside—if that is not a contradiction—and has little appeal in it-self; but the broken line of the Wall calls for careful observation and some powers of deduction, for unlike Hadrian's Wall this was an earth-work with a broad ditch and much of it has been levelled or over-grown. It linked Forth with Clyde, a distance of thirty-seven miles. One of the most massive sections is in the grounds of Callander House, east of Falkirk, and can be seen from a car passing along the main road; but the portion which Dr. Douglas Simpson rightly finds most impres-sive is near Camelon, at a Victorian house called Watling Lodge, and Dr. Simpson's comment is that 'the education of no Scotsman is com-plete until he had visited this site'. It is not the Wall alone which is so impressive here, but its commanding situation, the sense which one has of an Imperial frontier; and Sir George Macdonald many years ago suggested that this Wall, following the heights and seen from far off in the north, may have had a certain significance as a symbol of Roman might. The east end of the Wall was at a promontory in the sea not so far from Kinneil House, by Bo'ness, and Kinneil actually comes from a Celtic word meaning 'the end of the wall'; but there is little left of the structure there and the chief relic is a carved stone slab about nine feet long in the National Museum of Antiquities with a beautifully cut inscription in Latin to the honour of Antonine, done by the Second

Legion. It is a distance slab, set up at Bridgeness to commemorate the completion of a section of the Wall. The Second Legion moved to Scotland probably just before the building of the Wall by Lollius Urbicus about A.D. 143.

I have said this is an industrial countryside, or large parts of it are, but this does not mean it is of no interest to the non-technically minded visitor. Indeed, the present focus on industrial archaeology is sharpening interest in a type of bygone which has been too long neglected. Ruined palaces and abbeys and battlefields of long ago are only one kind of historic site; the hand-skills of a nameless populace were the means by which kings wielded their power and generals won their victories. Relics of technical progress have been valued so little that they tend to be much rarer than works of art, and already it is becoming hard enough to find significant things dating even from as recent a time as the Industrial Revolution. It was this event, or chain of events, which transformed Scotland from a centuries-old state of proud poverty to one of some prosperity, and enabled the Scots to exert a major influence on the world's development. Falkirk was one of what would now be called the 'growth-points'. Ore-smelting had always been a Scottish industry, the ore being taken to the forests which supplied the fuel, mostly in the Highlands. One of the key discoveries of the Industrial Revolution was that coke was better than charcoal for the purpose of smelting iron. Here in the waist of Scotland were vast supplies of coal for making coke lying beside deposits of iron ore. The man who pioneered the new industry was an Englishman, Dr. Roebuck, who had studied medicine at Edinburgh University, turned to chemistry and set up a sulphuric-acid plant at Prestonpans in East Lothian. Near Falkirk, on the little River Carron, he discovered the perfect site for an iron foundry, with coal and ironstone to hand, and an ample supply of that water-power which, as few now realise, was the main motive force of the Industrial Revolution. The Carron Ironworks was established in 1760. Within a decade or two it could supply anything in iron from a kitchen-grate to an anchor, and its cannon, notably the small guns which became known as 'carronades', were contracted for by every government in Europe. Unlike some other historic monuments, the company is still in business. So are some of its great rivals which followed hard upon its success. Perhaps, however, the most monumental physical relic of the revolution

1 *Hopetoun House*

of this time is the Forth and Clyde Canal, which links the eastern firth at Grangemouth with the western at Bowling. Building from 1768 to 1790, it can be said to have played an even more significant part in Scottish history than did the Antonine Wall, which runs so nearly parallel with it.

Another relic of industry, not likely to interest archaeologists, occurs mainly eastwards of Linlithgow. This takes the form of immense shale bings now so overgrown with rose-bay willow-herb and other things that they look like natural features. They are the products of the shale-oil industry, now in decline. I draw attention to those strange mounds in the first place because strangers are inevitably curious about them, and in the second because they drew attention to an important epoch in prehistory. The shales represent immense deposits of primeval mud, and the oil extracted from them was the organic residue of plant and animal life once mingled with the mud. The shales, then, were laid down in a huge tidal lake. The shellfish which inhabited it have left their shells behind them as a layer of limestone up to thirty feet thick, known hereabouts as Burdiehouse limestone. The lake sank and a forest of great trees grew above it and decayed, forming the coal measures on which the prosperity of mid-Scotland was built. Above the coal is rock, probably volcanic, so that a period of eruptions may have destroyed the forests. More forests grew upon the rock, and in turn became coal. Then the land sank again and the sea flowed in. Swamps followed, with fantastic tree-forms, inhabited by fierce monsters, a time chronicled in the rich deposits of the Carboniferous Limestone with their massive coal-seams. Finally came more eruptive activity, and the mounds of lava survive in the Linlithgow and Bathgate Hills.

The Bathgate and Riccarton Hills lie due south of Linlithgow. A pleasant day on foot can be spent in exploring parts of them, because the roads lead nowhere in particular and cars are few, and also because these hills contain some intensely interesting features. They are in themselves rather delightful, with heaths and thickets and patches of pine forest, so that even if the highest point, The Knock, is only just over 1,000 feet, they seem remote. Close against The Knock is a by-road which passes Cairnpapple, which is one of the most remarkable prehistoric sites in Scotland. It bears at first sight a resemblance to the domed top of one of those underground gun-emplacements which defended the Maginot Line, and the most casual eye would recognise it to be man-made even if H.M. Ministry of Public Building and Works had not made this obvious by tidying up steps and walls. Cairnpapple is a site which has been occupied over a vast period of time. As it stands, it is a Bronze Age burial-place, and urns and skeletons have been found belonging to different phases of this period; but perhaps a thousand years earlier than this a Neolithic temple was built here, and then again the Beaker Folk erected a stone circle with massive monoliths. These people dug a grave out of the rock and made a burial probably of some importance, since the site was a significant one. It is not difficult to understand the appeal of the hill to those early peoples. In a country where communications were difficult and dangerous, vantage points from which one could see distant places had an importance far greater than the mere romantic appeal of the view.

Barely a mile from Cairnpapple, in a sheltered hollow, lies Torphichen. Easy of access though it is from Linlithgow or Bathgate, or indeed from Edinburgh, this village is off the beaten track and too little visited. The focus of interest is the Preceptory Church of the Knights Hospitallers of St. John, founded by Malcolm IV in the twelfth century. Only a few fragments from that time survive, among them the archway in the west screen wall of the crossing. The rest of the building ranges from the thirteenth to the sixteenth centuries. The parish church, of the seventeenth century, occupies the site of the old nave. Architecturally, the preceptory is remarkable as one of those curious Scottish churches which, about the fifteenth century, adopted a secular, even military look, and what is left of Torphichen could almost be a baronial keep in which some eccentric owner had installed Gothic windows. There are two details worth looking for because they bridge the intervening centuries for anyone looking at them. One of the vault ribs in the north transept carries a Latin inscription to the effect that a member of the Order, Sir Andrew Meldrum, between 1432 and 1439 had safe-conducts to permit him to travel to Rhodes, Flanders and to England. The other detail is a scratched diagram on the west wall of the south transept, a builder's working-drawing for one of the vaults. There is always an odd satisfaction in coming upon evidence of how an individual dead and forgotten for centuries spent a few minutes over a problem which we can share with him.

Eastwards from Linlithgow, a loop can be thrown around a half-dozen or so places with a wide variety of appeal, and which can be seen with ease in a long summer's day. The only uneventful part of the journey is the first ten or a dozen miles along the Edinburgh road. The first point of interest is Kirkliston on the border of Midlothian. This is an ordinary enough village, and even the church does not seem to hold much promise; but it is one of those disconcerting Scottish churches with a severely nineteenth-century Presbyterian look which on closer inspection reveal a much longer history. It is almost startling to come on the south doorway, which, in spite of its worn and weathered state, is at once beautiful by reason of its Norman archway, and it is listed as the finest example of late Transitional work in the country. There are other Transitional details, and in time one looks with a kindlier eye even on the seventeenth-century additions. On the south side of the church is the burial vault of the Dalrymples, Earls of Stair, and the remains include Elizabeth Dundas's, original of Lucy Ashton in *The Bride of Lammermoor*. But only three or four miles to the north is a tiny church which is one of the two or three choicest of its kind in Scotland. This is Dalmeny. It is the most complete Norman church north of the Border. Here again the south door is the loveliest feature, with arcading very like that at Leuchars, and sculptured detail which makes it, in the view of Dr. Richardson, 'one of the best-preserved picture door-heads in Britain'. The interior is as charming as the exterior, the little sculptured corbels making a perfect foil to the simplicity of the rest, and when the light falls aslant into the tiny, raised sanctuary the effect is much more dramatic than the scale would seem to warrant. Dalmeny dates from about 1160, and the only major modification has been the tower, which collapsed and was rebuilt by the parish minister himself not so many years ago.

This countryside is dominated by the looming shapes of the two great Forth bridges. The approach-ways to the road bridge, more perhaps than the bridge itself, seem to draw the human tide into them and leave the pre-existing landscape and its features stranded and curiously remote. For those who can detach themselves from those baleful M-ways, there is a great deal of interest in and about Queensferry, from Dundas Castle with its fifteenth-century tower and beautiful seventeenth-century sundial with staircase to the little Barnbougle in the grounds of Dalmeny House where that great Prime Minister the fifth Earl of Rosebery probably wrote his books and speeches, and where his wonderful library still is. But I will point the way instead to the side-road which leads to the village of Abercorn, a few miles west of Queens-ferry. Cut off from the world by farmland and some magnificent stands of trees, Abercorn is entirely in another century. It clusters round its church. Again one can detect a Norman door, but the church is sub-stantially seventeenth-century. The most arresting thing in it is the Hopetoun family loft, perhaps the best example there is of a laird's loft and designed by Sir William Bruce, who built Kinross House. It has retiring rooms and a 'squint' enabling the family to know when it was time to end their refreshments and return for the sermon. Much less dominant is the Binns Aisle where old Tam Dalyell, to be mentioned presently, sat with his family. In the vestry are fragments of cross-shafts, probably coeval with the famous Ruthwell and Bewcastle crosses, which may be dated to the seventh century. Abercorn is men-tioned by the Venerable Bede, and it is tempting to see these stones as marks of the coming of Christianity from Northumbria to Nechtan, King of the Picts, described by Bede in A.D. 710.

Close by Abercorn is the most spectacular mansion in Scotland, Hopetoun House. Here we have a building in which it is hard to dis-cover any native element whatsoever, although it was built by Scottish architects. It is severely classical, yet strangely it was not conceived or built all in one piece. It was begun by Bruce, whose work ended in 1703, and carried to completion by his pupil William Adam, father of the more famous Robert. Robert, indeed, and his brother carried on with the interior work when their father died in 1748. Robert was a close friend of the Hopetoun family, and the second Earl's brother was with him in Italy on the tour during which the architect built the foundations of his fame, and it is probable that some of the Hopetoun furniture was made in Italy to the designs of Robert Adam. The house contains a worthy collection of paintings, among them a Rubens and three Van Dycks, and is built in one of the most gracious of settings. It belongs to the Marquess of Linlithgow.

The other laird who sat in Abercorn church, Tam Dalyell, had his home only a mile or two westwards. There are two low hills called the Binns, and on their slope is the House of the Binns, an early seventeenth-century mansion with romantic castellations added in the nineteenth. Its most notable structural feature is the magnificent plaster ceilings of Charles I's day, Italianate in style though with a fine rendering of the Royal Arms of Scotland. General Tam Dalyell, who looks out of more than one portrait, was the scourge of the Covenanters; but this adherence to the Stewart cause as against the Covenant, which has darkened his memory, tends to blot out the virtues of a tremendous personality. After Worcester he was cast into the Tower, escaped to the Continent, helped to reorganise the Russian armies and was rewarded by the Czar. This earned him his name in Scotland of the 'Bluidie Muscovite'. In 1681 he raised the companies of dragoons which were to become known as the Royal Scots Greys from the grey uniforms with which Tam Dalyell fitted them out, not from the dapplegrey horses which in modern times they rode. He was in every sense a legendary figure. One of the more picturesque if not more credible legends is attached to a marble table shown in the House of the Binns. This table was found in a nearby pond one dry summer in mid-Victorian times. Its finding went to corroborate the old tale that when General Tam played cards with the Devil and won, the Devil threw the table at him and it fell in this self-same pond.

The last place on this summer's-day circuit from Linlithgow is only a short distance along the road which goes north past the Binns. It is in fact the old port of Linlithgow, at Blackness. In the fifteenth century it had a harbour full of shipping, important enough for an English fleet to burn it in 1481, and in the eighteenth and nineteenth centuries it had some repute as a bathing-resort. Now it is a dreary village on the brink of mud-flats in which a hundred years ago someone sank a bore to a depth of 231 feet without striking bottom. It is the castle which is the only thing of interest left here, and that with its ordnance depot from the outside looks dull enough; but one must penetrate even the sixteenth-century outer-works to come to the core of the original castle built around the time the English fleet made its descent on the harbour. It is essentially a harbour defence fortress. Built on a narrow point of rock jutting into the sea, the castle itself is in plan, as the Ancient Monuments Commission describes it, like the deck of a ship, the old central tower representing the main-mast. In those days the sea came close to the walls on two sides, with a moat protecting the third. The

walls have large ports splayed for cannon, and it must have been a difficult place to take. In 1548 the French held the castle, part of Henri II's
gentle pressure on the Scots to consent to the marriage of Mary and the
Dauphin. In 1572 it was used to 'bank' temporarily the 50,000 double
ducats which was Mary's dowry from France. Her son, James VI, used
it as a prison for stubborn ministers of the Kirk who opposed him, and
John Knox's son-in-law was thrown into its dungeon for refusing to
condemn the Assembly.

five

Edinburgh
and the Lower Forth

To explore Edinburgh one should begin with the Castle. There may be a temptation among guides to keep the Castle as a climax, but it is the key to so much that it is a mistake to keep it for the last. Approach it, however, not by the usual route of The Mound, but by the more circuitous way of Castle Terrace and Johnstone Terrace. Where the first joins the second, go slowly and look well at the mass of rock towering above. Do it for preference with Geikie's classic *Scenery of Scotland* in one hand, for this is the perfect example of those 'igneous masses' mentioned early in my first chapter, those immensely hard extrusions from primeval volcanic vents which survived the volcanoes themselves and breasted the movement of the ice-mass of a later age. We have seen how history was built around just such another strong place, at Stirling. This rock is the very core of the Scottish capital.

Looking from the bridge where Johnstone Terrace overpasses King's Stables Road, one can in fancy best divest the rock of its accretions and view it at its most stark. This is Dunedin—the fortress on a hill, or perhaps in the place called Eidyn. The first of the ancient records of it is not in any Scottish source, but in the *Gododdin*, the celebrated sixth-century Welsh epic. The Anglian version of Dunedin is Edineburg, and as Lothian became for a time a part of Northumbria it was not unnatural to link the name of the fortress with Edwin, the Northumbrian king of the seventh century, although there are no grounds for doing so. Not until early in the eleventh century did Dunedin truly become a Scottish fortress, and when Norman knights filtered into Scotland they

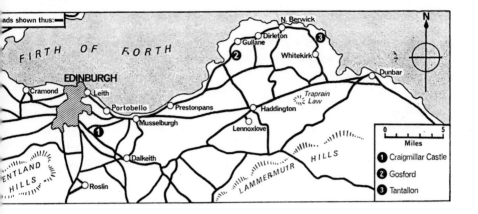

called the fortress on the rock the Maidens' Castle, *Castrum Puellarum*.

When the rock has been seen from below, it is time to climb to the Castle Wynd and so on to the Esplanade. This wide mustering ground well below the summit of the rock is spacious enough to accommodate a whole town's community in early times, and no doubt this formed part of the *oppidum Eden* referred to in the *Pictish Chronicle*, *oppidum* being used in the sense of a fortified town. The Esplanade is the beginning of the long tail of rock and detritus which the protecting crag of the rock itself shielded from the action of the ice-age glaciers, and it was on this tail that the medieval town of Edinburgh grew.

The Castle unfolds dramatically. Drawbridge and gatehouse, if theatrical, are modern; but once inside one goes back in time as one climbs to the summit of the rock. Towering above the narrow entrance-way is the great parapet of the Half-Moon Battery, built in 1574 to dominate the town three hundred feet below. The approach-way rises quite steeply, narrowed between the formidable wall of the Inner Barrier and the commanding height of the Forewall Battery, until it passes through the defences of the Portcullis Gate, constructed by the Regent Morton. From the gatehouse the causeway emerges on to the open terrace of the Argyle Battery, from which there is a first glimpse of the superb prospects to be had from the rock. Another sharp turning climb past the Governor's House takes the approach-way through Foog's Gate, a seventeenth-century addition, into the Citadel itself, the ancient core of this fortress. Over against the skyline is a tiny building which is the oldest in Edinburgh. This is St. Margaret's Chapel.

It is the remnant of a group of buildings associated with Queen Margaret, demolished and lost sight of before and during Cromwell's time, and the Chapel was rediscovered by that pioneer of Scottish archaeology, Sir Daniel Wilson, and restored in 1853. Wilson believed the Chapel to be the oratory of Margaret herself, where she heard of the death of her husband, Malcom Canmore, in 1093; but probably little of the existing Chapel is hers, and it is likely to have been built rather by one of her sons in her memory. The rounded interior within rectangular walls and the carved chancel arch are characteristically Norman work, almost the only such in Edinburgh. This area of the summit is called the King's Bastion. Apart from the view, which on a clear spring day with snow etching the peaks may embrace most of the more southerly tops in the Grampian range, the other focus of interest on the bastion is 'the great iron murderer called Muckle Meg', the cannon known as Mons Meg. This is a fifteenth-century iron bombard weighing five tons, casting an iron ball of 1,125 pounds to a distance of 1,500 yards, or a stone shot nearly twice as far. This piece, possibly cast at Mons in Flanders, demonstrates the immense power of ordnance even in the century of Flodden. The oak carriage is a replica of the one used with the gun at the siege of Norham. The gun lay for a time in the Tower of London; but Sir Walter Scott and others made strong representations which resulted in the return of the gun by sea in 1829.

On the south-east edge of the summit platform of the rock is a group of old buildings. The oldest of them, the St. David's Tower, is immured in the Half-Moon Battery, and the existence of this fourteenth-century block was suspected and confirmed only a few years before the First World War. This tower was finally reduced by a siege in 1573. Two early buildings survive more or less complete, however, forming two sides of what is known as Crown Square. The Great Hall, or Banqueting Hall, has been extensively remodelled, since for two centuries it suffered hard usage as a barrack and hospital; but it still possesses a fine hammer-beam roof and contains a varied collection of weapons including a number of steel pistols often described as Highland, but actually made by a man named Bissell, probably a Birmingham gunsmith, in imitation of true Highland pistols, for the use of the new Highland regiments raised for the British army after the echoes of Culloden had long died away. Its neighbour, the Palace or the King's

Lodging, is a fifteenth-century structure with some later details. This was in fact a royal residence at various times, and royal arms and ciphers appear in several places, although one display of the Royal Arms executed by the King's Master-Mason was completely obliterated by Cromwell's decree. The sovereigns associated with the Palace begin with Mary Queen of Scots. She gave birth to her son, the Prince who became James VI and I, in a room only a few feet square with one small window overlooking a precipice. The monograms of Mary and James— like all else in the room probably repainted in 1617—appear with the birth-date, 19th June, 1566, and this prayer:

> LORD JESU CHRYST THAT CROUNIT WAS WITH THORNSE
> PRESERVE THE BIRTHE QUHAIS BADGIE HEIR IS BORNE,
> AND SEND HIR SONNE SUCCESSIONE TO REIGNE STILL
> LANG IN THIS REALME, IF THAT BE THY WILL
> ALS GRANT, O LORD QUHATEVER OF HIS PROSEED
> BE TO THY GLORIE HONER AND PRAISE SOBIED.

It is a grim commentary on the times that the Queen who had known the stately châteaux as wife of the Dauphin should have her confinement in this closet, and no doubt it was fear of her beleaguerment in a hostile world that brought to mind her distant ancestress, St. Margaret, dying here in the same fortress with her enemies all about her, for she is said to have asked for Margaret's head to be brought her from the tomb in Dumfermline, as a relic for her to put her trust in. It was an unhappy omen. Not only did Mary herself lose her head, but Kirkcaldy of Grange who a few years later defended the Castle in her name lost his on a scaffold below the battlements, and the last royal occupant of these apartments, Charles I, fared no better.

In the nearby Crown Room lie the Honours of Scotland, the Scottish regalia. These precious things might well have been in the Tower of London with the rest of the regalia, for one of Cromwell's captains was within inches of them when they were spirited out of Dunnottar Castle during the siege, and although they were returned to Edinburgh Castle they were lost sight of until 1818, when Sir Walter Scott and a few other antiquaries made a search. They are less spectacular than the regalia in London, but in some respects more interesting. The Scottish crown is older than any of the others by far. Scott, indeed, held that it dated back to the Bruce's time, with the addition of the arches; but it is in fact the arches which belong to an older crown, and the fillet, which rests on the brow, was 'casten of new' by James V in 1540, and he also added the mound and cross *pattée*, as the cipher IR 5 demonstrates. The jewels are also older, and they include pearls from the River Tay. The gold used for the crown in 1540 by James Mosman, who did the work, is probably Scottish gold. I have set out the case for this claim in another book.* The sceptre was a gift from Pope Alexander VI to James IV in 1494, but it also was largely remade, by an Edinburgh goldsmith called Adam Leys, in 1536. James V seems to have had a passion for making the symbols of his sovereignty more massive, for the refashioned sceptre weighs much more than the original gift. The sword of State is another papal gift. Julius II gave this fine ceremonial weapon to James IV in 1507. The sword-belt did not come back after the Dunnottar episode, but was discovered in a garden wall in 1790 and remained with the Ogilvies of Barras, descendants of the keeper of Dunnottar, until it was restored to the Castle in 1893. Likewise the original cushion on which the crown rested did not come back to Edinburgh until 1905, and it is now shown with the regalia, although the crown lies on a modern cushion.

The west and north sides of the Crown Court are completed not by historical buildings, but by buildings which nevertheless have historical significance. One of these is the Scottish United Services Museum, which illustrates Scottish military and naval history by a wide range of exhibits including regimental uniforms and badges, weapons, medals and ship-models. The other building is the Scottish National War Memorial. Sir Robert Lorimer set out to erect a chapel-like structure which would take its place in the familiar skyline of the Castle, yet merge with its surroundings, and he incorporated an old barrack wall. Architect, builders and artist-craftsmen worked as a team rather in the medieval manner of which Lorimer was such an accomplished student. The quality of the stonework, metalwork and stained glass in itself pays tribute to the fallen, and the Stone of Remembrance rises from an outcrop of the black basalt of the Castle Rock itself which pierces the floor of the shrine.

The medieval town clusters along the ridge which drops away to the Palace of Holyroodhouse, and the street which leads from the Castle to

Scottish Gold and Silver Work, Chapter 5.

Holyroodhouse is known as the Royal Mile. It is one of the most fascinating streets in the world. At the same time, it poses an absorbing problem. While many of the old houses remain, many were knocked down in the nineteenth century and replaced by tenements, and for generations large portions of the famous Mile were a slum. The City Fathers made a laudable assault on this unhappy state and have cleaned it up, and they are now in process of saving and renovating the older buildings. The problem which poses itself is how to treat the gaps in the ancient street: whether to fill them with buildings in the medieval manner, as for example has been done in Nuremberg, or with structures in contemporary idiom, or with some sort of compromise. To me, the happiest aspect of the problem is that as the work progresses the amount of medieval or at any rate seventeenth and eighteenth-century masonry seems to be revealed in greater measure. Rehabilitation is radical. The renovated houses are turned into shops and dwellings, and the time may come when the former slums are again the fashionable residences they once were. Meanwhile, no stranger should look with dismay at house-fronts washed pink or green or prinked out with smart paintwork, for it was the grim, grey tenements of Victorian days which were out of character, not the 'new look' of the 1960's. Even a piece of steel-and-glass modernity here and there would be less improper than the stony tenements, for change and adaptation are of the very spirit of the Scots vernacular architecture.

No one understood the organic nature of Scots architecture better than Sir Arthur Geddes, whose Outlook Tower rises at the head of the Mile. Geddes has been called the father of town-planning, and his advice was sought in every backward country from India to Mexico; but the Outlook Tower was his 'sociological laboratory' and at the same time the symbol of his ambition. Here the eccentric professor of botany expounded his concept of Place-Work-Folk, the method of analytical survey on which he based his ideas of planning, and here he delighted in illustrating his concept by using the camera obscura in which visitors may still see a panorama of the city reflected. With his cloak and beard, he was perhaps one of the last of Edinburgh's picturesque geniuses—he died at Montpellier only in 1932—and he used to boast that the Tower was his burglar's lair, presumably where he cracked the safe of knowledge, in imitation of a notorious neighbour of a century earlier, Deacon Brodie, around whom R. L. Stevenson wrote a play. This individual lived about a hundred paces down the street, in the Lawnmarket. Brodie was a respectable citizen by day, and a burglar by night, and when fate caught up with him in 1788 he fled to Holland, was caught there and returned and hanged on a gallows of an improved type devised by himself. The Lawnmarket is rich in fine houses. One of the finest is Gladstone's Land, now the headquarters of the Saltire Society and a property of the National Trust for Scotland, typical of the tall, narrow 'lands' of the Old Town. The ashlar frontage is seventeenth-century, but there are extensive sixteenth-century portions, and there are some splendid painted ceilings, one of them identical with a ceiling in the Palace at Culross. To appreciate the character of these houses, however, one must penetrate the closes and go into the inner courts. Riddle's Court is a good sample. Patched and decrepit as it is, it is a dramatic piece of late-sixteenth-century building. Further on is the house of Bailie McMorran. If the exterior is forbidding, it contains rooms which were obviously once very fine, so that it is no surprise to learn that Birrel's Diary records on 2nd May, 1598, James VI and his queen, Anne of Denmark, dined here with the Duke of Holstein, an occasion of 'great solemnity and merriness'. It is typical of the Old Town that these memories of the Renaissance mingle with the very different splendours of the eighteenth century, for it was to Riddle's Land that David Hume came in 1751—'a house of my own . . . and a regular family, consisting of a head, viz. myself, and two inferior members, a maid and a cat'. Here he began his *History of England*. Opposite is the entry to Lady Stair's Close, a spacious courtyard with high seventeenth-century houses to east and south. The Dowager Countess of Stair was a woman of great character, no mere queen of fashion although she owned the only black servant in the town, and her story became the basis of Sir Walter Scott's tale of *Aunt Margaret's Mirror*. There has been a good deal of rebuilding in this close, but its high rooftops and turret stairways give a fair impression of how the Old Town had to build skywards on a restricted site and anticipated Manhattan Island. The full stature of those extraordinary dwellings is best viewed from the back, where they overhang the slopes to the north. Every wynd and close here, and indeed from here to Holyroodhouse, is encrusted with tales tragic and comic, and the wooden balconies and stairs which once clung to their fronts were close witnesses of central events in three centuries of Scottish history. For in Scotland, even the monarch was not remote from the town's common life, so that Mary Queen of Scots could have flowers thrust upon her on her first triumphal entry and with equal ease be jostled on the causeway when she returned in shame, a prisoner, after the defeat of Carberry.

Below the foot of the Lawnmarket is the High Kirk of St. Giles, still commonly enough called St. Giles' Cathedral although only during five years out of the eight centuries of its existence could it be properly so-called. Eight centuries may seem too much to claim, as there is only one certain Norman fragment and perhaps a few others reused, but there was a fine twelfth-century porch until the end of the eighteenth century. From the outside there is nothing medieval but the tower and its beautiful crown steeple, because in 1829 a mock-gothic 'restoration' encased the ancient masonry. But the bulk of the fabric is in fact of the fourteenth and fifteenth centuries, although it must have come through fire at the Burnt Candlemas of 1335 and at the hand of Richard II during his invasion of 1385. The church grew rather in the Scottish manner, here an aisle, there a chapel, by contrast with English regularity, and the interior at first sight presents a picture of stern and gloomy caverns, of lowering vaults supported on massive columns, and only as the eye grows accustomed to this twilight does it begin to see the sculptured detail and the tattered battle-flags. One must peer at some of the detail to savour the full richness of this church: at the boss which still bears the M for the Virgin Mary, despite the iconoclasm of Knox, at pier-capitals bearing the badges of great names, such as Archibald, fourth Earl of Douglas and Duke of Touraine, or the Duke of Albany, Governor of Scotland from 1488 to 1520—all these in the North Aisle. The chapels reflect varied aspects of the kingdom's life. The first of Scottish printers is commemorated in the Chepman chapel, the chaplaincy of which was confirmed by James IV only a few days before he fell at Flodden. In the Preston Aisle one thinks of William Preston of Gorton who in 1454 bequeathed to the church the arm-bone of St. Giles himself, obtained in France. St. Eloi's chapel, close to the north entrance, was endowed by the town guilds of craftsmen. St. Giles' might have grown in grandeur under the endowments of the town's growing prosperity; but the sixteenth century, which began

auspiciously with the appointment of the poet Gavin Douglas, trans-
later of the *Aeneid* into Scots, as provost of the church, soon brought
the disaster of Flodden and in little more than a generation Mary of
Guise's French troops were trying to fend off the Reformation in the
streets around and soon Knox had mounted the pulpit of St. Giles'.
Knox shared its roof with schoolmasters, clerks and prisoners, for it
was made to serve half-a-dozen purposes, and for a time Kirkcaldy of
Grange put a garrison and guns in the tower in the Queen's name. Here
her son, James VI, was to wrangle with Presbyterian theologians, and
it was his son, Charles I, who for a few short years from 1633 turned
church into cathedral and fomented the riot during which Jenny Geddes is supposed to have thrown her stool at the Dean. But it might almost be said that the sombre splendours of the church have prevailed
over Presbyterian iconoclasm, for to-day even the normal service in
St. Giles' is not without pageantry, minister in the scarlet gown of a
royal chaplain, choir in matching scarlet, while on such occasions as
a procession of the Order of the Thistle to its modern but exquisite
chapel or a dedication service of the Edinburgh Festival there is a return to pomp and circumstance which must trouble the great Reformer
whose burial-place is marked in the street a stone's throw from his
church.

St. Giles', although the High Kirk, stood in no splendid isolation.
Houses jostled it on all sides, and the wooden stalls known as the
Luckenbooths—the locked, as opposed to the open booths—reared
against its north wall. Here and hereabouts were the shops of the goldsmiths, among them the seven-feet-square booth of George Heriot,
goldsmith and lender of money to James VI, where to vie with a costly
fire of aromatic logs which he had seen at Holyrood he cast on his fur-
nace before the eyes of His Majesty a bond for £2,000 Scots which he
had lent to the King. Here, too, at a later time, were the shops of Allan
Ramsay, wigmaker and noted poet, and William Creech, the book-
seller, where such men of letters as Smollett came to gossip. A heart let
into the cobbled pavement marks the site of the old Heart of Midlothian, or Tolbooth, which in the latter part of its four centuries of use
served as the town prison, and in that function was described by Scott,
in whose time it was demolished, in *The Heart of Midlothian*. Behind St.
Giles' is the Parliament Square. Near the Knox's reputed grave in the

Square is a remarkable leaden statue of Charles II seated on a charger, erected in 1684 in a position chosen for a statue of Cromwell. On the south side of the Square are the Law Courts, further victims of the 'improvers' of 1829. Here the Scots Parliament met until the Union. Happily, the improvements did not extend to the Parliament Hall, a dignified chamber 122 feet long under a hammer-beam roof. It is now the meeting-place of the advocates who, when the courts are in session, pace up and down on the parquet in wig and gown consulting with clients or, in winter, clustering about roaring fires in the three splendid fireplaces. Among many busts of Scottish jurists in the Great Hall the most noteworthy is Roubiliac's statue of Lord President Forbes of Culloden.

Wynds and closes also honeycomb this section of the Royal Mile, the High Street, and the lofty frontages are interrupted here only by the old Royal Exchange, now the City Chambers. They cannot all be noticed here, but one which should certainly not be missed is Advocates' Close, a deep tunnel giving on to steps and stairs dominated by a magnificent turret staircase. This close was named after a Lord Advocate, Sir John Stewart of Goodtrees, and in the eighteenth century many lawyers had their chambers here, including the original of Counsellor Pleydell in *Guy Mannering*. On the other side of the street is the Tron Kirk. Now celebrated mainly as a place where crowds 'see in' the New Year, this church, built by the King's Master-Mason, John Mylne, in 1642, no longer functions as a place of worship and its continued existence has been in dispute. Some two hundred yards further down, the High Street narrows. Here, at the Netherbow Port, the burgh of Edinburgh ended and the burgh of Canongate began. Just at this point, where the street narrows, is the projecting sixteenth-century dwelling called John Knox's House, with Moubray House behind it. The Knox attribution can be traced no further back than 1784, when the Hon. Mrs. Murray claimed in a guidebook that the Reformer 'thundered his addresses to the people' from its bow-window, and in Knox's day this house was owned by James Mosman and his wife Merion Arres, whose bearings are carved on the front. Mosman was a supporter of Queen Mary and was executed with Kirkcaldy of Grange. The real importance of the house lies in its being the only dwelling on which the old timber galleries survive.

13   *Edinburgh: St Giles' Cathedral—the Choir*

'Gate' in old Scots is a street or way and has Dutch and Swedish parallels, and the Canongate takes its name from the canons of Holyrood Abbey. It survived as a burgh separate from Edinburgh until 1636, when it came under the jurisdiction of the magistrates of the capital, but for long after this it retained its independence in many things and retained its own trade-guilds. Its craftsmen were among the most skilled in Scotland, as a glance at the Galloway mazer in the National Museum of Antiquities will demonstrate. It is in the Canongate that the major rehabilitation schemes have been proceeding since 1952, and there is promise that something like the picturesque and colourful street of past times will be reconstituted. This was a favourite quarter with the Scots nobility in the seventeenth century, and indeed before and after it. Moray House, now a teachers' training college, became the property of the Countess of Moray in 1645 but was built by her mother, Mary, Dowager Countess of Home. Cromwell lived in it in 1648 and held levees there, and before and after him Charles I and Charles II were visitors. Traditionally the balcony is that on to which Lord Lorne, later Duke of Argyll, stepped with his bride, Lady Mary Stuart, and their wedding guests to watch Montrose pass up the street to his execution at the Tolbooth. The gardens behind the house were once famous—'scarcely anyone would believe it possible to give so much beauty to a garden in a frigid clime'. The chief beauty of the house now lies in its plaster ceilings on the first floor, especially Lady Moray's reception-rooms and the Cromwell room. Two buildings which between them preserve the old atmosphere to perfection are Huntly House and Acheson House, on either side of the delightful Bakehouse Close. Huntly House seems to have been a timber house reconstructed in stone in the sixteenth century, and is now used as the City Museum, where a great variety of bygones and material relative to the town's history are displayed. A copy of the National Covenant is perhaps the most important of all these. Acheson House was built in 1633 for Sir Archibald Acheson of Clonekearney, Co. Armagh, and it is one of those parts of the Canongate rescued and restored by the late Robert Hurd, the architect who perhaps more than anyone in his generation was dedicated to the reconstitution of the Old Town. Acheson House is now occupied by the Scottish Craft Centre, which fosters and markets the best in craftsmanship to-day. Directly opposite Huntly House is the

Canongate Tolbooth. Dating from 1591, when it was described as 'great and sumptuous', it served both as court-house and prison. Next to it is the Canongate Church. Described by Smeaton, for some reason, as architecturally 'inconceivably tasteless', this church is in fact quite charming and its front, except for the classic portico, is lifted straight from Holland. Its burial-ground is rich in great names. Here Robert Burns erected the stone over the grave of the young poet to whom he owed much, Robert Fergusson. Other tombs range from those of Adam Smith, David Allan, the portrait-painter, and Horatius Bonar, the hymn-writer, to the last resting-place of Dr. Gregory, whose notorious Mixture may well have been concocted in his house in the Canongate. I will pick out only two other features in this street so full of things worth mentioning. One of these is the house at No. 81, where a stair-tower carries this inscription:

CVM VICTOR LVDO SCOTIS QVI PROPRIVS ESSET
TER TRES VICTORES POST REDEMITVS AVOS
PATERSONVS HVMO TUNC EDVCEBAT IN ALTVM
HANC QUAE VICTORES TOT TVLIT VNA DOMVM

This is the house known as the Golfer's Land, and the reference is to one John Paterson, who was invited by the Duke of York, later James VII, to partner him in a game against two Englishmen who declared that Englishmen could play golf as well as any Scots. The Englishmen were beaten on Leith Links, mainly by the fine play of Paterson, a poor shoe-maker, who was given the wager played for and with it built his house. He placed his arms on it, but the motto has perished. Appropriately, it is said to have been 'Sure and Farre'. The other feature which must be described is White Horse Close. This is possibly the most pic-turesque surviving piece of old Edinburgh, and it is one of those features of the Royal Mile which have been judiciously restored. It consists of a long, paved courtyard surrounded by small dwellings, and it has more timber features than are usual in Scotland. It dates from the seven-teenth century. The delightful building at the far end has a forestair which divides right and left to give access to the upper floor and has twin gabled projections of wood and plaster supported on timber cor-bels. This was the celebrated White Horse Inn which has a place in *Waverley*, and Prince Charles Edward's officers had their quarters here.

The name of close and inn is said to derive from the colour of the palfrey which Queen Mary rode.

At the foot of the Canongate, flanked on one side by an interesting little building called the Abbey Strand, are the gates of the Palace of Holyroodhouse. These are the Abbey Lands, an ancient regality, and carry the right of 'girth' or sanctuary, a right which 'has bene inviolablie observit . . . and that in all tymes bigane past memorie of man', to quote from a Supreme Court edict of 1569. The Abbey of Holyrood was founded in 1128. Tradition has it that David I founded it in gratitude for the appearance of a miraculous cross which saved him from a stag on this spot, and the stag's head with a cross is the burgh crest of the Canongate and was the town-mark of her goldsmiths. Tradition seemed to be discredited when, in 1911, an apparently Celtic church was unearthed under the Abbey, but this is now accepted as the remains of the original Abbey Church. The Church was rebuilt on a grander scale later in the twelfth century and added to in the fourteenth and fifteenth centuries. It was burnt by Hertford's men in 1544 and the lead stripped from the roof by the same hands three years later. Charles I had it repaired for his coronation in 1633, and later it became the Chapel Royal for the Palace; but in the middle of the eighteenth century it was found that the roof-timbers had decayed, and a builder posing as an architect tried to replace the timber roof with stone slabs, and the extra weight brought about the collapse of the roof and the ruin of the Church. Only the ruined nave now remains above ground. The Royal Commission on Ancient Monuments of Scotland describes the façade as 'one of the finest early medieval compositions in Britain'. Perhaps because it is half-hidden behind the shoulder of the Palace, this lovely Abbey Church is not seen at its full value and is not the place of pilgrimage which Melrose is. It has some of the finest architectural detail of its period in Scotland, and its sculptures include a particularly fine early Gothic group above the west portal, done in the thirteenth century, representing the heads of seraphs in the Heavenly Choir. It is a building of great nobility, even now when so many of its walls and columns are no more than flat stones breaking the lawns where guests wander at royal garden parties.

There is a drawing in the British Museum showing Edinburgh in 1544, the year of the Earl of Hertford's invasion, and the Palace of

Holyroodhouse is shown as a high-turreted building which Dr. W. Douglas Simpson has seen as French in style. This was the Palace which Mary knew. Little of this remains, for after the Restoration Charles II decided to rebuild, employing Sir William Bruce of Balcaskie as architect, and Robert Mylne, the King's Master-Mason, undertook to do the work for £54,000. The new Palace was built around an inner quadrangle, now a lawn. Architecturally, the only distinguished aspect is the façade, which at either end culminates in a projecting tower. The north tower incorporates James IV's tower and is the only substantial part of the earlier Palace, although even this was modified by Mylne. The Royal Arms on this tower are replicas of those removed by Cromwell's troops, but I recall the emotion shown by a group of the Maquis visiting the Palace during the Second World War when they detected the cross of Free France in the arms of Mary's mother, Marie de Guise-Lorraine. This tower contains the 'Historical Apartments'. These have been modified since the time of Mary Queen of Scots, and in general the furnishings are of the seventeenth century. A little turret-stair communicates between Darnley's apartments on the first floor and Mary's on the second, and there is no good reason why the assassins of Rizzio should not have used this stair as tradition maintains. The floors of Mary's audience chamber and bedroom have been raised three feet since her time, and Bruce overpanelled the original walls, but the tempera frieze exposed above the fireplace in the audience chamber Mary may have seen, in brighter tones, and the ceilings with their heraldic panels and royal initials could certainly have witnessed the tragic Queen and heard the accusations of John Knox. Adjoining Darnley's chambers on the first floor is the Long Gallery or Picture Gallery, a handsome room seen at its best with the stir and colour of an evening function, but noted chiefly for its 'portraits' of a hundred Scottish kings, from Fergus I—'330 B.C. !'—to James VI, which Jacob de Witt contracted to paint in two years, 1684 to 1686, at a salary of £120. They are not masterpieces, and Hawley's dragoons did not improve them in their rage over their defeat at Falkirk, but they have a certain naïve appeal. It was here that Prince Charles Edward held the ball described in *Waverley*. There are works of art of much finer quality in the State Apartments. The tapestries especially are notable and include four fine sixteenth-century Brussels pieces on the State staircase and four relating the story of Diana woven in Paris to designs by Toussaint Dubrieul.

The spread of Edinburgh beyond its narrow ridge of the Royal Mile began long before the day of Lord Provost Drummond. As early as the fourteenth century the town had crept down into the valley to the south. The focal points equivalent to Holyroodhouse and the Castle were a Dominican friary established in the thirteenth century and a Franciscan house on higher ground to the west where the Kirk of the Greyfriars now is. Between these grew up the Cowgate. Looking at this rather grim canyon of a street, it is hard to credit Alesius' description of it as 'where the nobility and chief men of the city reside, and in which are the palaces of the officers of state, and where is nothing mean or tasteless, but all is magnificent'. Not much of interest is left now in the Cowgate except the Magdalen Chapel. This was put up just before the Reformation that prayers might be offered for the soul of Mary Queen of Scots, for the founder and his wife, and for the deacon and masters of the Hammermen Craft. The Magdalen Chapel is in fact the Chapel of the Hammermen, among whom were craftsmen ranging from blacksmiths to goldsmiths, and the link between craft and church was in no way broken after 1560. The tailors had their hall close by, also in the Cowgate, and Candlemakers' Hall is in Candlemaker Row just round the corner. The Cowgate debouches on to the wide space of the Grassmarket, where sales of cattle took place first instituted by the monks of the Greyfriars. The most interesting house is close to where the West Bow comes down into the market. At one time this was Graham of Claverhouse's dwelling, and from it he could look down on the gallows where so many of his Covenanting foes were despatched.

In what were once the productive gardens of the monks Old Grey-friars Kirk was built in 1612. To it more than a century later the New Greyfriars was added. Architecturally the churches are of no great distinction, but the churchyard is a hallowed spot, because on 26th February, 1638, the National Covenant was signed here, copies being brought out and laid on a table-tombstone. Ironically, in 1679 the Covenanters beaten at Bothwell Brig were brought here in chains and kept in the open from June until November because no prison could contain them. The churchyard itself is a monument of Edinburgh society over four centuries. Beginning with George Buchanan, the historian, whose grave is lost, the list of great men buried there includes Alexander Henderson, the Covenanting leader, George Jamesone, the portrait-painter, Allan Ramsay, Henry Mackenzie, William Carstares, a host of political figures headed by Duncan Forbes of Culloden and other great lawyers in plenty, among them a Vice-Chancellor of England and Master of the Rolls. Here also lies George Heriot, father of the gold-smith. And over the wall, surrounded by terraces and lawns, is Heriot's Hospital, founded by his son. Heriot *fils* had Christ's Hospital in mind when he endowed this great foundation, the building of which began in 1628. Although the architect, William Wallace, built in a past fashion, he produced a splendid composition in Renaissance style with mark-edly Scots detailing, and the chapel, which faces the entrance to the grounds, has windows which are reckoned as the finest examples in Scotland of the last phase of late Gothic. Cromwell commandeered the the school for a hospital and tried to retain it, but in 1659 the establish-ment was dedicated with thirty scholars clad in the statutory doublets, breeches, stockings and gowns of sad-russet cloth. To the west of Heriot's grounds is a passageway known as the Vennel, and this is worth investigation because in part it is flanked by the largest surviving section of the old city wall erected in haste by the citizens after the disaster of Flodden.

We turn to modern Edinburgh, for which the University may be taken as a significant starting-point. Strangely, Edinburgh's is the youngest of the four older Scottish universities. The Toun's College was founded in 1582. Its buildings grew around the site of the Kirk o' Field, the house blown up to accomplish—or to cover up—the assass-ination of Darnley, but by the later eighteenth century the buildings were wholly inadequate for the growing number of students, and in 1785 the Town Council was empowered to rebuild the College. It had the good judgment to commission Robert Adam to do the work. The site is not ideal, because it is fronted on the east by the South Bridge, a main north–south artery, which in these days of further expansion poses a problem; but Adam's ambition to create a great public build-ing would have been achieved here but for his death in 1792. Econ-omies were demanded. After long delay, William Henry Playfair was entrusted with completion of the building. He achieved what is still a fine composition, but he had to modify Adam's plans drastically. None of the interior is of Adam's design, but he could hardly have bettered the splendid Upper Hall of the Library, a gallery 138 feet long with lofty, moulded ceiling and glorious side-lighting. But this great building around a quadrangle, now called the Old Quad, is no more than the hub of a university which has expanded both materially, so that it is now scattered over half the city and indeed beyond its limits, and as a massive cultural force. Its famed Medical School is centred on the New Quad near by. And the university quarter embraces other institutions allied in the spread of learning. A group of great libraries includes the beautiful Signet Library, belonging to that exclusive body of solicitors called the Writers to the Signet, and the National Library of Scotland adjoining it. The National Library is one of the five copyright libraries in the British islands, which have a right to a copy of every book published in this country, but in addition to its vast reference collections of books it possesses many treasures in the fields of documents and ancient manuscripts. Among these are innumerable letters, one of them a touching epistle from Mary Stuart as a small girl to her mother. Then neighbouring the Old Quad is the Royal Scottish Museum, the largest museum outside London, the entrance hall of which is the most impressive piece of Crystal-Palace architecture left in the country. This national institution possesses extensive collections of material illustrating the decorative arts of the world in all ages, natural history and geology, and science and technology.

Surely one of the most dramatic confrontations in any city in the world is to be had by walking the few yards from the foot of the Lawnmarket, in the Old Town, to the foot of Bank Street. There, spread out below, lies the New Town. A little more than two centuries ago there was a reedy loch, the Nor' Loch, and beyond were fields and farms and copses and a road called the Lang Gait approximately where Princes Street now goes. By 1750 even the extension of the town to the Cowgate and its environs could not relieve pressure in the restricted accommodation along the Royal Mile and conditions in the wynds and closes were becoming appalling. A long-projected bridge, the North Bridge, was thrown across the east end of the valley to the north of the town and the Nor' Loch drained. Lord Provost Drummond had urged the need to build a better town on this northern ridge and to improve the link with the Port of Leith, and the bridge was the first step. About

14   *Edinburgh: White Horse Close*
15   *Edinburgh: North side of Charlotte Square*

1760 James Craig drew up a plan for a town of broad, intersecting streets, a gridiron plan, with its main street along the crown of the ridge, named after the King, George Street. A parallel street along the edge of the valley he called St. Giles' Street, but to George III this roused memories of a narrow lane in the City of London and the name was changed to Princes Street. Building proceeded, at first slowly, from east to west, and the first and finest part of the New Town reached its climax with Robert Adam's design for Charlotte Square, which terminates George Street in the west as St. Andrew's Square does in the east. This is a superb piece of planning in the classic manner, and in neoclassical style, and there can be no doubt that this great western square is the finest thing of its kind in Europe. There are squares more tremendous in impact, but none quite so perfectly proportioned or so exquisitely finished. Princes Street has achieved more popular fame, because of its spectacular prospect; but unless the civic pride of Drummond's day returns, and millions are sunk in a scheme to drive out the intruding chain-stores and replace them with enterprises more worthy of one of the noblest street-sites in the world then Edinburgh will surely lose one of its most celebrated assets.

In spite of conditions in the Old Town citizens were hesitant about moving to dwellings on the exposed ridge to the north. The houses being erected there had grandeur, but the streets were wide and draughty, and indeed the New Town, for all its model plan, has never been as functional or weather-wise, as the Old. When the idea caught on it became the fashionable thing to move, but it wrought a social cleavage between the two towns. From the Lord Advocate and the Lord Justice-Clerk down, the legal profession migrated. So did the gentry, great and small. The wealthier merchants copied them. Even literary men took the step, among them David Hume, and when the great sceptic's house-wall was chalked by an unknown passer-by with the ironic title of 'St. David's Street' the name stuck and so the street is still named.

With the coming of the nineteenth century the New Town expanded rapidly. Farms and fields were consumed as they are by urban expansion to-day, but at least they were replaced by monuments to real civic pride. The Heriot Row charters date from 1803. Moray Place and the other magnificent circuses and crescents which crown the bluff overlooking the Water of Leith followed twenty years later. Country mansions like Drumsheugh were forced to make room for palatial urban mansions, leaving nothing but their names; and the new houses had rooms of the most perfect proportions, with elegant plaster ceilings and mantelpieces, many of them following Robert Adam's designs, or at least his taste. Several generations of cultured men and women were to inhabit them before rising site-values and the lack of servants below stairs turned them into offices and hotels. In those rooms historic events were planned, in them men who spoke in broad, rugged Scots penned many of the classics of English literature, made basic discoveries in medicine, even laid the first broad foundations of what was to be the atomic age. There was wit as well as learning. The Assembly Rooms in George Street housed balls and routs as gay as any in Europe, despite the retreat of Court and Government to the south. The Golden Age lasted for half a century and more. This was the Edinburgh of Cockburn's *Memorials* as it was the Edinburgh of Lockhart's *Life of Scott* and of Robert Louis Stevenson's memories. But as R. L. S. knew better than any it was a Jekyll-and-Hyde of a city, with dark slums spreading in the Old Town abandoned by the society of the New and men of learning and wit not above making use of the world of Burke and Hare. One must remember too that even architecturally the two towns are not neatly divided, but are interlinked. George's Square has been a delightful Georgian precinct tucked away behind the Old Town—I say 'has been' because the University has incomprehensibly demolished much of it to erect multi-storey teaching blocks which could have gone elsewhere. And overlooked by the classical New Town the old Dean Village lies in a wooded hollow where at least one ancient craft is still practised beside a dark reach of the Water of Leith and the hum of the city's traffic seems to come from far off.

There is another town within Edinburgh. At the east end of Princes Street, close to where Robert Adam built one of his masterpieces, the Register House, a narrow, busy street drops towards the broad thoroughfare of Leith Walk, where not so many years ago trace-horses waited to help pull the great drays and waggons uphill from the port of Leith. Leith has a strange remoteness from Edinburgh. It has always resented Edinburgh's domination. Even John Knox in his *History of the Reformation* records the 'haitrent and contentioun betuix Edinburght

and Leith'. A town of tough seafarers and fishermen, it had at one time
a big trade with the Low Countries and France, and by the seventeenth
century was described as opulent, yet in the same century a visitor
wrote of it as the 'slave' of Edinburgh. Leith therefore felt it had good
reason for resisting annexation, but this took place at last in 1920, and
now there is not even a burgh boundary visible or the old intriguing
change at Pilrig from one tramway system to another to rouse a visitor's
curiosity about this ancient and, by tourists, neglected port. Its narrow
streets have an atmosphere quite different from its neighbour's, in part
compounded of the flavour of ship-chandlers and mills. Its old and
historical buildings are few, and grow fewer. Appeals for their preser-
vation follow one upon another. Lamb's House, in Waters' Close, has
been saved. Tradition connects it with Mary Queen of Scots' arrival in
Leith in 1561, although it looks to be of the early seventeenth century,
modified in the eighteenth. Pilrig House at the moment of writing
awaits an offer to save it from the breaker. At Granton, neighbour port
to Leith, commercial expansion threatens Caroline Park House with its
glorious ceilings and wrought-ironwork. Historically, Leith is a town
of ghost-sites, and the eye of the archaeologist is needed to conjure up
the Citadel or the King's Wark, begun by James I as part-palace and
part-armoury.

In any country it is necessary to turn to museums and galleries to
study some of the choicest treasures of its culture. I have made
occasional reference, not only in this book but in its companion volume
on the Highlands, to objects in the National Museum of Antiquities.
This red sandstone building is at the east end of Queen Street. Its
exhibits cover in material form the whole range of Scotland's story,
from Palaeolithic times down to the nineteenth century. It is perhaps
more fitting to mention individual pieces in their context, as I have
done already; but I would stress here that this is the principal collection
of Scottish bygones, archaeological and historical, and that most significant finds or relics are preserved here. In certain fields such as metalwork, textiles, glassware and ceramics, there are large collections also
in the Royal Scottish Museum, but there they are shown in a world
context. Under the same roof as the National Museum is the Scottish
National Portrait Gallery, with its unrivalled collection of likenesses
of men and women prominent in Scottish history. The general work

of Scottish painters of the past is to be found in the National Gallery
of Scotland, close to Princes Street. Here are major works by Raeburn,
Ramsey, Wilkie and many others. But it should be said at the same time
that this gallery contains a small but choice collection of paintings from
all schools, including masterpieces by Rembrandt, Vandyke, El Greco,
Titian, Constable, Turner and the Impressionists.

In the space available one cannot do more than indicate a few of the
more interesting localities in the environs of the city. Cramond village,
at the mouth of the River Almond, is worthy of a visit. Not only has it
a fine medieval bridge, but close by Cramond House there is a late
fifteenth-century tower, and Craigcrook Castle in Blackhall, which is
on the way to Cramond, is a delightful piece of seventeenth-century
vernacular. Cramond itself was an important Roman station, and in
the eighteenth century the building of the manse laid bare various remains. An altar from Cramond is in the National Museum, bearing an
inscription: *To Jupiter, Best and Greatest, the Fifth Cohort of Gauls, under
the command of the Prefect Minthonius Tertullus, in glad, willing and well-
deserved payment of a vow*. A longer expedition may be made with the
first objective Craigmillar Castle, three miles south of the city. This is
one of the most spectacular ruins in Scotland, clustered about a late
fourteenth-century tower. The curtain walls are particularly impressive. The castle was destroyed by Hertford in 1544, but was rebuilt by
its owners, the Preston family. Mary is said to have plotted the murder of Darnley here, and Little France on the Dalkeith road probably
commemorates her French followers. Circling by Dalkeith and New-
battle Abbey, a family mansion of the late Marquess of Lothian which
is now a college of adult education, and by Hawthornden, built on to
an older tower by the poet, William Drummond, in 1638, one comes
to Roslin. Roslin Chapel is one of the most remarkable ecclesiastical
buildings in the country. William de St. Clair, Earl of Orkney, is recorded in the *Scotichronicon* as building this collegiate church, in the
fifteenth century, but only the choir was ever completed. It became the
burial-place of the Sinclairs, who were said to have been placed in the
vault in full armour. But the chapel is notable chiefly for the sculptured decoration, carried to a pitch of elaboration found nowhere else
in Scotland.

The main road into East Lothian is the A.1, the main road to the south. It has a rather devious beginning, turning this way and that. The old road goes by way of Portobello, a town of seaside boarding-houses popular in Glasgow Fair Week. There is not a great deal to tempt one to go by this route except perhaps the compulsion of the curious name, which was given the town by its first inhabitant, a sailor with Admiral Vernon's expedition to Portobello in Panama in 1739. Guidebooks record that Hugh Miller, the pioneer geologist, shot himself in Tower Street a century ago, and it is worth remembering that the collections made by this extraordinary, self-taught man from Cromarty are preserved in the Royal Scottish Museum. Musselburgh, the next town, has much more attractive features. The most striking building is the tolbooth, with its patently Dutch steeple and its attractive forestair. It was destroyed by Hertford, but rebuilt in 1590. East of the tolbooth the street becomes spacious, with some attractive old dwellings. East of this again are the gates of Loretto, where the boys' public school occupies the site of the convent of Our Lady of Loreto, also destroyed by Hertford but in any case discredited for fraudulent 'miracles'. The school possesses one splendid Renaissance building in Pinkie House, dating from 1613, celebrated particularly for the painted ceiling of its long gallery. Musselburgh boasts it is older than Edinburgh, and as its burgh status can be traced to the reign of David I the boast is not altogether empty, and when the Riding of the Marches takes place the Town Champion rides out armed cap-à-pie. A narrow lane on the south side of Musselburgh High Street leads uphill to one of the most pleasing retreats in the vicinity of Edinburgh. This is the village of Inveresk, now in part a preserve of the National Trust. It is an old village, with some good seventeenth-century houses. When 'Jupiter' Carlyle was minister here the manse became a den of literary lions, for Carlyle was an open-minded Moderate and warmly approved his play-writing colleague, the Rev. John Home, author of *Douglas*, and admired Mrs. Siddons and even entertained the unbeliever David Hume. Inveresk's story goes back much more than two or three centuries, however, for it was an important Roman station. Now not much remains but some foundations and the corner of a hypocaust in the grounds of Inveresk House, but a great deal was unearthed in former times, and Mary Queen of Scots commanded the bailies of Musselburgh not to demolish anything and Elizabeth's envoy, Randolph, took much interest in the finds.

The route eastwards by the shores of the Firth is not so obviously picturesque, but it is the main avenue of approach to Edinburgh from the south and its fields are soaked in history. Battlefields are numerous. At Pinkie, Hertford defeated the Scots army in 1547. At Prestonpans in 1745, Charles Edward beat the royal army under Sir John Cope, a victory still remembered in the song of 'Hey, Johnnie Cope'. Historical buildings are not so numerous, but the little collegiate church of Seton, close to the main road, is beautiful though incomplete. Aberlady Bay presents a glorious, wind-swept panorama, and behind a high barrier of bent trees lies Gosford House, seat of the Earl of Wemyss and March. Robert Adam was commissioned to build it but the house was not completed until nearly a century after his death. The Lord Wemyss who decided to build here did so because he liked golf. The dunes and links along this coastline are the real cradle of golf in Scotland. One great course succeeds another. Golf, like the local steeples and church-bells and brass chandeliers and silver beaker communion cups, is one of the relics of the trade bond between eastern Scotland and the Low Countries. It was established in Scotland by the sixteenth century, and Mary was reviled for playing with Bothwell on the links at Seton only a few days after Darnley's killing. The senior club in the game is not, as most people suppose, the Royal and Ancient at St. Andrews, but the Honourable Company of Edinburgh Golfers, who formerly played on Leith Links but now have their home on the great championship course of Muirfield, near Gullane. The silver club presented by the City of Edinburgh in 1744 for annual competition, at the suggestion of 'several Gentlemen of Honour, skilful in the ancient and healthful exercise of Golf', can be seen in the clubhouse.

Beyond Gullane lies one of the most attractive villages in Scotland, Dirleton. In layout it has rather an English look, with houses fringing a stretch of open ground like a village green. They are sheltered from haars off the Firth by a good screen of trees. There are pretty gardens and one or two excellent inns and an attractive church. It is all evidence of a good life, a fertile soil and able husbandry, and indeed it is on record three hundred years ago that nowhere around could grow wheat such as grew in 'Lordship of Diriltoune'. To complete the picture, a castle presides over the village, and it looks all that a medieval castle should look. A good deal of the original castle built in the thirteenth century remains, stronghold of the Norman family of De Vaux brought in by David I. Wallace held out here in 1298 against Edward I. It was the bribe offered to Logan of Restalrig to take part in the Gowrie Plot against James VI, and when the conspiracy failed the King gave the castle to Sir Thomas Erskine. It was both a strong place and an agreeable one to live in, with a pleasaunce and a bowling-green. North Berwick, a couple of miles on, is in sharp contrast to Dirleton. In spite of much new building it still looks the rather sophisticated Edwardian watering-place, and an air of exclusiveness clings even now around the golf-course. However, there is some historic ground under the comfortable villas. A fragment of the Auld Kirk down by the harbour could be the kirk associated with one of the most notorious witch-craft cases in Scottish history, the affair of the North Berwick Witches, who were brought to trial for plotting the death of James VI on the high seas. King Jamie had a lifelong interest in the witch-cult, and followed this trial eagerly. It could well be this kirk which Agnes Samson had in mind when she confessed to being present when the Devil— 'a muckle black man'—preached to a congregation of witches and warlocks. But North Berwick's greatest historic monument is Tantallon Castle. This could be called the most spectacular castle in Scotland. Built on the neck of a small promontory, it consists of three huge towers joined by curtain walls. Its rear needs no fortifications: it is formed by sheer precipices falling a hundred feet into the sea. To add to its strength there is a moat before it, and the only access was across a drawbridge and under a portcullis commanded by battlements which could throw a devastating fire on the attacker. As to supplies, only a close blockade could prevent these coming in by sea. This was one place which Hertford in 1544 decided he had not the artillery to reduce. It was a Douglas stronghold, and Scott brings it into the pages of *Marmion*. Gunpowder eventually did defeat these massive defences, for in 1651 General Monk and his Ironsides bombarded it for two days and his 'battering-pieces' at last breached the wall and the stones collapsed into the moat and bridged it. The sea-front of North Berwick is dominated by the Bass Rock. A block of basalt 350 feet high, it is another of those volcanic plugs which strew the Lothians area but it happens to occur in the sea. The Bass is of interest both to historians and to ornithologists, severally or together, for the solan goose, of which this is one of the few breeding stations, has elicited comments even from such a notable as Charles II who, in spite of the fact that the bird was considered fare for kings, remarked that there were two things in Scotland which he heartily disliked, solan goose and the Solemn League and Covenant. Charles, perhaps influenced by his distaste for geese, turned the rock into a prison for Presbyterian ministers, who became known as the Martyrs of the Bass. Lauderdale was the instrument of this oppression, and as a result his repute in all Lothian was low indeed. The Bass was a strong fortress, and it was the last corner of Britain to recognise William of Orange as king of the realm; it yielded only when starved out by men-of-war.

Inland some miles from Tantallon is what might be called the ghost of one of the prettiest little churches in Scotland. Whitekirk was burned down by the Suffragettes in 1914, but the fifteenth-century church has been beautifully rebuilt and is still well worth a visit, partly because of historical documentation which includes an account in the Vatican Library describing how a holy well here attracted so many pilgrims that James I added to an existing chapel and called it the White Chapel. One of the pilgrims, in 1435, was Aeneas Sylvius Piccolomini, who became Pope Pius II. All his days he suffered from rheumatism, which he blamed on his barefoot pilgrimage to Whitekirk!

The port at which Aenius Sylvius landed may well have been Dunbar. Dunbar to-day is built of the Old Red Sandstone which weathers down into the rich red soil of this part of Lothian. Its older part is in its way picturesque, with alleys and closes off the High Street leading to the sea, but, the Town House excepted, there are few noticeably historic buildings apart from the ruinous castle down by the harbour. This fortress, jutting into the sea, was one of the strongest on the invasion route into Scotland. Such castles were more important to invaders than to defenders, who preferred to melt away and leave a region of 'scorched earth'; but the most famous siege of Dunbar occurred in 1338, when Montacute, Earl of Salisbury, with a mighty force invested the castle in the absence of its owner, the Earl of Dunbar. But Black Agnes, his countess, took command. She is said to have put on a suit of mail and deliberately exposed herself on the ramparts, and if a missile from the English catapults smashed into the stonework near her she ordered one of her ladies delicately to dust the spot with a handkerchief. She

defied all the ruses of the attackers, and by a ruse in return almost managed to capture Montacute himself. After six weeks a relieving force from the Bass penetrated the blockading fleet and brought supplies, which so disheartened the English that they raised the siege. In 1560 the French strengthened the castle. Mary Queen of Scots used it several times. She fled there after Rizzio's murder, and followed Bothwell there dressed as a page. There she got together her last army, which marched to Carberry and defeat. At last the Regent Moray reduced the place, and in 1567 it was 'demolischit and cassin downe utterlie to the ground'.

To return westwards by an inland route . . . After East Linton the road climbs a little to expose a wide spread of farming country bounded by the Lammermuir hills, but out of this rises another of those volcanic rock-masses. This is Traprain Law. There is not much to interest the casual visitor in this now, especially as a road-metal quarry is eroding it; but all these 'crag-and-tails' became islands in a waste of bog and bush and therefore attracted settlements of early man. Bronze Age man at least came this way, probably from the Low Countries, and fortified himself on heights such as Traprain. This might be the basis for the legend of King Loth, supposed to be buried under the Loth stone at the foot of the hill and sometimes credited with the origin of the name of Lothian. Traprain's main claim to fame, however, is the treasure found there in 1919, the richest hoard of treasure trove ever found in Scotland. The Treasure of Traprain, now in the National Museum of Antiquities, comprises about 160 articles of silver, Roman work of a high level of craftsmanship executed about the time of the Empire's collapse. Some of the vessels were broken deliberately, and the buried hoard had the appearance of loot. It may have come from some villa in Gaul, raided by those Saxons who were descending on the crumbling frontiers.

A few miles up the River Tyne we come to Haddington, the county town of East Lothian. A by-pass has left it with much beauty that might otherwise have been lost, and the High Street is a street of great character. There are good seventeenth-century houses fronting it, and a fine old bridge links the town with Nungate. Bothwell Castle, now ruinous, was until recently an attractive sixteenth-century town house which belonged to Cockburn of Sandybed. Haddington, athwart the road to Edinburgh, was sacked again and again: by King John, by Edward III, by Hotspur, by Hertford under orders from Henry VIII. Its pride was the parish church of Mary the Virgin, the Lamp of Lothian, as it is popularly though wrongly known. It is a splendid fifteenth-century church with a notable west window. At one time it had as many as eleven altars with such ringing names as Crispin and Crispianus and the Three Kings of Cologne. It contains a marble monument to the Lauderdales, and the man who committed the ministers to the Bass—he who was the L in Charles II's hated Cabal—lies in the vault below. Long after his death they said his guilt kept him from rest, as his leaden coffin changed its position in the vault, but the flooding of the Tyne might have something to do with this. The seat of the Lauderdale family, the Maitlands, was Lethington, a mile or two south of Haddington. It has changed its name to Lennoxlove, and in 1947 passed to the Duke of Hamilton. On land granted to Maitland of Thirlestane in the fourteenth century the present fifteenth-century tower of rubble was raised, and there were additions in 1626. The greatest of the line was William, famed as Secretary Maitland, whose qualities were such that Queen Elizabeth could call him 'flower of the wits of Scotland' while yet so faithfully did he serve her rival Mary that he died for it. The avenue of trees known as the Politician's Walk commemorates his strolling there deep in thought. The interior of the house mingles relics of the two houses of Hamilton and Maitland, and range from the day of Charles II to the Second World War and the strange descent of Rudolf Hess in Scotland. I will, however, concentrate on one group of relics. In the White Room is a portrait by Lely of Frances Stewart, Duchess of Richmond and Lennox, and also in the house are items of her furniture. Charles I's widow called Frances 'the prettiest girl in the world'. Pepys delighted in her, Evelyn wrote of her, she runs through the pages of the *Memoirs* of the Comte de Grammont, John Roettiers took her as model for Britannia on the coinage; but above all Charles II fell madly in love with her. When she died—she is buried in Westminster Abbey—she left her fortune to her cousin's son, Lord Blantyre, and with it the trustees bought the estate of Lethington and renamed it Lennoxlove. But it was not until about 1900 that here in the attic they found a walnut travelling chest containing what is probably the most magnificent French silver toilet service in existence, each constituent piece of which carries the monogram of 'La Belle Stuart', as she was called at Court. It could only have been a Royal present, a gift from the Merry Monarch himself. In recent years its owner sold it, but it was purchased for the nation and is on display in the Royal Scottish Museum, but it is such a masterpiece that it was sent on exhibition back to Paris, where it was made, and given a place of honour in the Salle du Roi in the Louvre.

six

Lanark and Clydesdale

Lanark in itself makes no great claim on our attention. It is an obvious choice as a base for exploring the county. It is a splended centre. It has long history. It is a prosperous market town. But when we look around it for the sort of feature which preoccupies us in this book little meets the eye except what a Victorian guidebook to the place describes as 'the County Buildings, erected in 1834–6 at a cost of over £5,000 . . . built in the Grecian style of architecture'. Even the monument to the local hero, William Wallace, is a statue done in 1817 by a local sculptor with no obvious genius.

Lanark's situation in itself, however, makes it quite certain, even if there were no records, that it must always have been a place of importance. It has a commanding position on high ground overhanging a bend in the gorge of the Clyde. There is water-power and richly productive land in plenty in every direction. Yet the only structure of real antiquity is the ruined twelfth-century church of St. Kentigern, southeast of the town on land originally granted by David I to the monks of Dryburgh. There may have been a fort in Roman times: certainly there is a Roman road at Collielaw and from Hyndford crannog not far away Samian ware in plenty has been recovered. But Lanark's chief place in history was won by Wallace, who is believed to have lived in the Castlegate. Here his brief, brilliant career began. The story goes that he and his friends had a scuffle with some of the English garrison in the street, that he escaped, that his young wife Marion Bradfute, heiress of Lamington, was brutally slain by the English sheriff, Hazelrig, and that

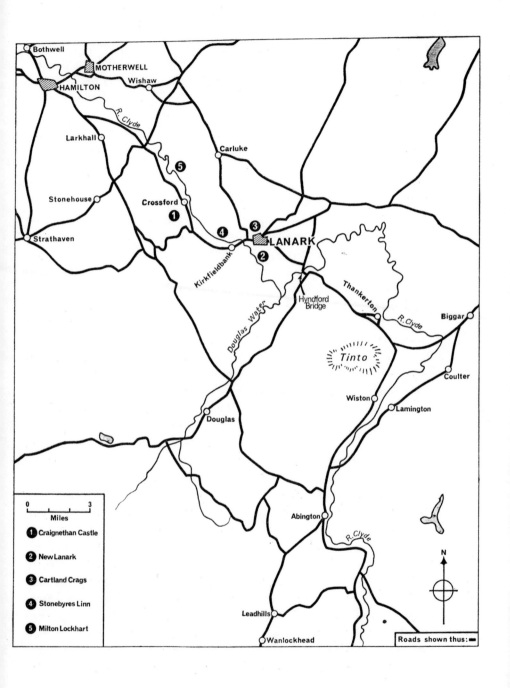

Bothwell

MOTHERWELL

HAMILTON   Wishaw

R. Clyde

Larkhall   Carluke

⑤

Stonehouse   Crossford

❶

Strathaven   ④ ❸ LANARK

Kirkfieldbank   ②

Douglas Water   Hyndford   Thankerton
                     Bridge   R. Clyde   Biggar

                                    Tinto   Coulter

                          Wiston   Lamington

Douglas

Abington

R. Clyde

                                                              N

0   3
Miles

❶ Craignethan Castle

② New Lanark

❸ Cartland Crags

④ Stonebyres Linn   Leadhills

⑤ Milton Lockhart
                        Wanlockhead   Roads shown thus:

in revenge Wallace and his friends seized the castle and slew Hazelrig. The town had its first charter from William the Lion. He gave it nothing more tangible, for although tradition claims that the silver Racing Bell of the town was his gift it carries the mark of the Edinburgh goldsmith Hugh Lindsay and the deacon's mark of Robert Denneistoune, which dates it between 1608 and 1610. Tradition is cherished, however, and the Lanimer Day celebration of beating the bounds is observed with enthusiasm every June. Essentially this is a town rooted deep in an agricultural community, and its old staple industry of hand-loom-weaving grew up against this background.

Textiles brought into being the town's near neighbour of New Lanark. South of the town, and deep-sunk in the valley of the Clyde, New Lanark is a social-historical monument of the first importance. In the first place, it underlines the great part played by water-power throughout most of the Industrial Revolution. Availability of a big head of water guided David Dale in his choice of what was an unpromising, marshy site for his mills in 1784, and to bring it to bear where he wanted it he had to dam the Clyde and drive a channel a hundred yards through solid rock. This channel was less a mill-race than a rushing canal, still an impressive thing in itself. His dwelling-houses were models for their day. He aimed to break the popular aversion to factory life by introducing amenities. Not until management passed into the hands of Robert Owen did prejudice and opposition dwindle—they did not die out—and Owen saw that re-education had to begin with the child, in 1806 founding what must have been the first infant school in the country. Backed by such men as Jeremy Bentham and Michael Gibbs, later a Lord Mayor of London, Owen bought the mills and turned New Lanark into what has come to be regarded as an experiment in socialism, and one which roused tremendous interest at the time. As one comes down the hill, it all looks a little forbidding. The dwelling-houses rise out of the depths with the air of barrack blocks. But a closer look shows the fine quality of the building, and the pedimented fronts of the mills loom behind against the hanging woods beyond the river with a curious dignity. It becomes easy to understand how it impressed distinguished visitors, what with uniformed workers and well-mannered children. And these buildings with their classical façades were as efficient as they were elegant, promoting an industry which, adapting itself to change, has survived to this day. Ropes and canvas are no longer the output, but have been replaced by modern synthetic fabrics. The great mill-wheels went nearly a century ago, replaced by steam power; but Dale's mill-race can still generate 650 horse-power and light and heat the mills electrically. A scheme is afoot, in the hands of leading architects, to rehabilitate the dwelling-houses and modernise them internally. There is some talk of an Owen museum. Indeed, I am told that the fact that Robert Owen is prescribed reading for students in America and Japan already brings many visitors from both countries to this leafy dell. The house where Owen lived and entertained many notable people is neighbouring Braxfield, once the home of Lord Braxfield the Lord-Justice Clerk, the 'hanging judge' who is a central figure in Stevenson's *Weir of Hermiston*. Not far off the Clyde roars over two of its most spectacular falls, Cora Linn and Bonnington Linn. Southwards, framed in the valley, rises Tinto.

Before considering Clydesdale I will give a page or two to the upper reaches of the river. What this region lacks in antiquarian interest, speaking relatively, it more than compensates for in wide horizons. By Hyndford Bridge and Thankerton, the road skirts the eastern slopes of Tinto. Little though it may look it, this is in fact the watershed of southern Scotland, for at this point the Tweed is only a few miles away from the Clyde, and Geikie has remarked that an adjustment of the gravel mounds at Thankerton would send the Clyde down to the sea at Berwick instead of at Dumbarton. Indeed, a writer in *The Angler's Companion for Scotland* once maintained that the presence of salmon in the Clyde above its highest fall of eighty feet could only be accounted for by the fusion of the upper waters of Clyde and Tweed under conditions of flood! Tinto is a landmark for many miles around. It is a conical hill more than 2,300 feet above the sea, an igneous mass smoothed by glacial action. It is more impressive at a distance than on close acquaintance, and the climb from Symington is featureless and without any of the rocky outcrops or heathy vegetation of Highland hills; but its name means 'hill of fire' and no doubt it bore signal beacons and perhaps Beltane fires in early times. There are many myths attached to it, some remembered in verses such as the well-known lines beginning 'On Tintock tap there is a mist'. A diversion east at Symington is worth while, to pass up the right bank of the Clyde by way of Biggar, Culter and

Lamington. It is not that these villages are of any particular note for their history or antiquity, but Scotland is not so rich in attractive villages that one may ignore these three. They are set in fine farming country, watered by pretty streams winding into the Clyde. Culter Fell and the Peebleshire hills lend them some shelter from the east. Biggar is more than a village, although most of it is contained in one street, which has good features, including a small bow-backed brig. In early times it was something of a feudal village, protected by the Flemings of Boghall, but in 1451 James V made it a burgh of barony. A Lord Fleming in 1546 built its collegiate church of St. Mary, last of the pre-Reformation foundations in Scotland. The kirkyard should be a place of pilgrimage for Liberals, since the evolution of the family name of, first, Gledstanes, then Gladstones, and finally Gladstone can be traced out among the tombstones. The grandfather of William Ewart Gladstone moved from Biggar to Leith about 1756. Culter—pronounced Cooter—is no more than it looks, a cluster of cottages in pretty gardens shaded by fine stands of trees. Lamington is equally pleasing. Its early eighteenth-century church, however, has a beautiful Norman doorway, and the link with Sir William Wallace's wife, Marion Bradfute, exists in Lamington Tower, where she is said to have been born, although its surviving remains scarcely date from her time.

At Abington the road joins the main south route, a new dual carriageway which has dispelled some of the atmosphere of upper Clyde. Here in the extreme south tip of Lanarkshire the hills crowd in on both sides, the burns from which the Clyde springs purling down out of the cleuchs. At Elvanfoot a side road climbs away up into rather dreary hills dominated by the Green Lowther. Among these hills lie the two highest villages in Scotland, Leadhills and Wanlockhead, at 1,350 and 1,380 feet about 200 feet higher than the highest of Highland villages, Tomintoul. Lead seems to have been mined in these hills since the thirteenth century, and still provided a considerable industry less than a century ago. Some silver was associated with it. But the romantic product of those dark, brooding hills was gold, and it may well have been gold from Crawfordmuir, in the shadow of Green Lowther, which was used for the Crown of Scotland, to which I referred in the previous chapter. The river gravels were shown to bear gold particles in James IV's reign, and at his son's marriage to Mary of Guise each wedding

19   *Lamington Church*

guest had put before him a cup filled with 'bonnetpieces' of Crawford gold, which were described as 'the finest fruits' of a barren moor. Something of a gold-rush developed at this time, and the very diverting story of it can be read in *The Discoverie and Historie of the Gold Mynes in Scotland*, by Stephen Atkinson, a manuscript in the National Library published by the Bannatyne Club in 1825. Elizabeth's nose for treasure was set-atwitch by what another writer described as 'God's Treasure-House in Scotland', and she sent her secret emissaries to try to abstract some of the gold without the King of Scotland's knowledge. Her celebrated miniaturist, Nicholas Hilliard, with a partner, actually obtained a licence to work the Scottish gold-mines from the Regent Morton; but perhaps the climax of the story is James VI's direction to Sir Bevis Bulmer to procure twenty-four gentlemen to put up the money for a new mining enterprise around Wanlockhead, the reward offered by the canny King to each being the bestowal of the title, 'Knight of the Golden Mynes'. Leadhills has other claims to fame. Small, remote and, in a hill-mist, bleak as it can be, it was the birthplace of Allan Ramsay, the poet, and of William Symington, who applied steam propulsion to drive a boat as early as 1788. Later Symington's *Charlotte Dundas* was the first steam vessel put to practical use, but an ungrateful government allowed him to die as obscurely as he had been born in Leadhills.

Returning northwards across the hills we come to the Ayr road and the Douglas Water. Douglas itself is not unattractive, but developments in the coal industry have not improved the amenity of the countryside, and they have destroyed Douglas Castle, which in its original form was the stronghold of the Good Sir James Douglas, friend of Robert Bruce. It was Scott's 'Castle Dangerous', only a small fragment of which survives. Douglas was killed fighting the Saracens in Spain. His body, and the casket containing Bruce's heart, were brought back to Scotland, and Douglas's canopied tomb may be seen in the chancel of St. Bride's Church, a twelfth-century foundation in the village. If the Bruce's tomb at Dunfermline is a place of pilgrimage, the whereabouts of Douglas's must be known to very few.

The Clyde valley proper is one of the two or three most favoured districts in all Scotland. Protected from north and east by higher ground, it stores the sun in a deep, rich soil well worked for hundreds of years. The river here flows slowly through a succession of black salmon pools. There are two seasons for coming here: in May, when the orchards are under clouds of pink and white blossom, and from the strawberry season on to September, when plums second to none in the world may be had by the basket straight from the growers' hands. Some of those gnarled old hands could put their signatures to cheques for five figures or even more, for to the strawberries and plums have been added tomatoes, although the tomato houses have done something to spoil the rural beauty of the valley.

The descent of Lanark Brae to the river, once hazardous, has been smoothed by the road engineers, and the new bridge at Kirkfieldbank provides no awful climax to the descent as the much more beautiful old bridge did. Where the Mouse Water flows into the Clyde the eye is drawn to the towering mass of Cartland Crags a mile away, where the Mouse, in spite of its modest name, seems to have gnawed a chasm through the Old Red Sandstone since the end of the Ice Age. The Crags afford a strong refuge, and the feature called Castle Qua may have been used in early times, or by William Wallace, whose reputed cave is lower down. Certainly the chasm was used by Covenanters for their conventicles. There is a Telford bridge over the Mouse, and below it is an older bridge often referred to as Roman; but although the Romans did explore this part of the country they carefully avoided making roads where the users of the roads could be ambushed easily, as O. G. S. Crawford has explained, and as they built their bridges of timber laid across stone ramps or abutments they were hardly likely to survive many centuries. Further up the glen is Jerviswood. It was the home of Robert Baillie, one of the pillars of the Presbyterian resistance to Charles II's attempt to reimpose episcopacy in Scotland, and a victim of his own honesty; for when questioned about complicity in the Rye House Plot he volunteered knowledge of an insurrection in Scotland and in due course was butchered at the market cross of Edinburgh.

Below the Mouse's entry into the Clyde is Stonebyres Linn, a once spectacular fall of seventy feet now reduced to pay for hydro-electricity. There have been descriptions of its 'horrid and savage aspect' going back to Pennant. It was the highest point on the river to which salmon could go, and their vain attempts to go higher at one time were a popular attraction here. Orchards and glass-houses alternate both on the flat land by the river and on the slopes above, and the cottage gardens are filled with flowers. The place-names of this valley—Hallhill, Hazelbank, Crossford, Stonebyres—have a rural simplicity which reflects the place. They are old but they have not the ring of antiquity and seem to belong to the romantic early nineteenth century, like most of the 'gentlemen's seats' in Gothic or Tudor or embattled taste which rise from fine sites on the wooded hillsides. Crossford is an attractive village. Like so many other names here it has an obvious origin, although the village cannot be so very old, as a seventeenth-century writer refers to a tryst 'att the Corseford boat . . . neer midway between Corhouse and Cambusnethan', as though nothing were there but the boat. The ford must have met the road up to Lee House, home of the Lockharts of Lee since the thirteenth century. The present house is a turreted mansion with a Gothic hall built in 1822 upon the remnants of the old Lee Castle. Simon Loccard fought beside Bruce and was knighted by him, and he it was who brought back the Bruce's heart from Spain. He also brought back an interesting relic, which he is said to have got as part-ransom from the wife of a captive prince : a dark-red stone described as set in a coin of Edward I, which became celebrated as the Lee Penny. It gained a prodigious reputation as a talisman with curative properties which it transmitted to water in which it was dipped, but it is no longer at Lee House.

Just beyond Crossford, and on the same side of the river, the Nethan comes down into the Clyde at Nethanfoot. A path leads up the side of the burn, for a mile or more, through hanging woods, to the castle of Craignethan, or Draffen as it used to be called, best known as the original of Tillietudlem Castle in *Old Mortality*. It is a promontory castle, high above the burn, with natural defences on three sides. Built in the sixteenth century when gunpowder already threatened traditional defence works, Craignethan has gun-ports enough to suggest something like panic measures, and one is left wondering what some of the targets could have been. But this is a very interesting castle, with the defensive tower of earlier times beginning to yield to a baronial residence, with its banqueting hall and minstrels' gallery. It was built by Sir James Hamilton of Fynnart, natural son of the first Earl of Arran, and as Sir James was Steward to the Royal Household and Superintendent of Royal Palaces and Castles, his own stronghold has a special appeal. He built both Falkland and Linlithgow palaces, and added to the castles of

Rothesay, Stirling and Edinburgh, so that he left a considerable mark on the land. James V attended here the wedding of Sir James's daughter Agnes with the Master of Somerville. The next James, ever a suspicious man, accounted the Hamilton family guilty of being mixed up in treasonable affairs, and in 1579 he held Craignethan forfeit and partially demolished it. The castle came back to the family a few years later, but they preferred their seat of Hamilton and Craignethan fell more and more into disrepair. Happily its decay has been arrested by the Ministry of Public Building and Works.

After Milton-Lockhart, where Scott chose a magnificent site for the mansion of William Lockhart, half-brother of his son-in-law and biographer, the Clyde winds tortuously through Dalserf to Garrion Bridge. The whole wide vale can be seen stretching away to the heights at Lanark. From this point the road begins to move away from the river and the horizon to the north grows grey with the breath of industrial Wishaw and Motherwell and Hamilton. Hamilton provides another example— they are all too common in this country—of how mineral wealth can destroy the character of a town. Old engravings of Hamilton depict splendours which are no longer even memories, for the town is on the verge of the Scottish Black Country. A first encounter with the town from the south is encouraging, for the High Parks still have all the appearance of a nobleman's estate, with the Avon winding through the centre of them towards the Clyde. On a crag overhanging the Avon are the ruins of Cadzow Castle. It has one of those romantic situations which Scott could not resist . . .

> '*When princely Hamilton's abode*
> *Ennobled Cadzow's Gothic towers,*
> *The song went round, the goblet flowed,*
> *And revel sped the laughing hours.*'

This sixteenth-century fortress is remarkable in several ways, but Stewart Cruden has pointed out that it is unique in Scotland in its salient battery tower, sunk into the ditch which it commands, a feature which has a close parallel at Schaffhausen on the Rhine. There seems to have been an older castle on the site, but this was probably built by the second Earl of Arran, when it became a Hamilton stronghold. The Earl was made Duke of Châtelherault, a French title which still belongs to the Duke of Hamilton; and on the opposite bank of the Avon is a building called Châtelherault, said to have been copied from the château of the name in 1732, although clearly intended to be little more than a romantic decoration in the park. The park possesses some ancient oaks sometimes associated with the old Caledonian Forest, and Cadzow is celebrated also for its herd of native white cattle, the only survivors in Scotland of the wild breed represented in England at Chillingham. In later years, however, the ducal home was changed to Hamilton Palace, which stood in the Low Parks, not far distant from the Clyde. The passing of Hamilton Palace is a sad chapter in the Scottish story. There was an old building on the site when the Duke commissioned the Palace in its final form, completed in 1822, but the architect completely altered it and achieved what was recognised to be one of the most imposing neo-classical structures in the kingdom, its frontage 264 feet long. The erection of the building was quite an epic in its way. Each of the twelve columns of the portico was hewn from a single stone in a quarry at Dalserf and drawn to the site by thirty horses. This was building in the grand manner, made possible by great riches. But more remarkable than the building were the art collection and the library. The paintings included works by Rembrandt, Titian, Velasquez, Rubens, Giorgione, Vandyke, Poussin and many other masters. There were many treasures, books, plate and other things, which had belonged to that extraordinary man, William Beckford, the founder of Fonthill and author of *Vathek*, whose daughter married the tenth duke, Alexander. Among the furnishings were pieces which had belonged to Marie Antoinette. It was indeed the premier art collection in Scotland. But in 1882 and again later everything came under the hammer. Some things remained in the Hamilton family, but they were relatively few. Paintings, furnishings and books are dispersed across the world. One of the most prized possessions of the Metropolitan Museum of Art in New York is an Italian Renaissance table from the Hamilton Palace collection. One touching relic which was not sold is the Turner watercolour of Fonthill in the late Duchess's bedroom in Brodick Castle on the isle of Arran, for Arran was a Hamilton possession and the Duchess spent some of her childhood in Hamilton Palace. Scotland lost what should have been part of her heritage at the sale of 1882. The treasures the family was forced to sell should have been purchased for the museums and galleries of Scotland. And the crowning disgrace occurred in 1927, when subsidences due to coal-workings caused the Palace to be pulled down after just over a century of its existence. All that is now left is the ducal Mausoleum, a strange, deserted building reputedly modelled on the castle of St. Angelo in Rome. The weird beauty of the echo in its empty chapel is fitting comment on the fate of the Palace and its splendours.

Below Hamilton Low Parks the Clyde is crossed at Bothwell Bridge, a reconstruction of the old brig for the possession of which Covenanters were defeated by Monmouth and his Royalist army in 1679. The old brig was a narrow, hump-backed affair, and Hackston of Rathillet and Hall of Haughead with three hundred men held it for a time, but they had to yield and a terrible massacre followed. A mile to the north lies Bothwell, an oasis in the conurbation of Glasgow. Bothwell has a long history, and the old collegiate church of St. Bride can still show a ruined choir and sacristy dating from 1398, when Archibald the Grim, Earl of Douglas, founded it. It contains some interesting stone sculptures, including triple trefoil sedilia and some heraldic work, with refined detail in the style of this time, carried out in red sandstone. A minister of Bothwell in the eighteenth century had a distinguished daughter, Joanna Baillie, the song-writer and dramatist, who could claim descent from Sir William Wallace. Close by, on the river's edge, is Bothwell Castle, one of the most massive and powerful strongholds in the kingdom. Its main feature is the great donjon-tower, 65 feet across and 82 high, the innermost defence in a system of formidable defences. It contained considerable accommodation, with an octagonal central hall having timber rib-vaulting, and the large finds of medieval pottery fragments show that it was more than a fortress; but it is as a military structure that it has most appeal, seeming quite impregnable. However, there is no such thing as an impregnable fortress. Dr. Douglas Simpson points out that the very conception of the donjon is defeatist, implying successive withdrawals and eventual starvation. The Scots did in fact take Bothwell from the English after a fourteen-month siege in 1298–9, and Edward I recaptured it in 1301, displaying his usual interest in engines of war by bringing up 'Le Berefrey', as Mr. Stewart Cruden tells us, 'a prefabricated wheeled tower of great size and ingenuity which was conveyed some twenty miles in thirty wagons to the scene of its operation'. When Sir Andrew de Moray, its owner, finally won the tower back from the English in 1336, he cast down half of it into the river.

Across the river from the castle was Blantyre Priory, described by Dorothy Wordsworth, and in *Scottish Chiefs* associated with Wallace's escape from the English. It brings us full cycle back to Lennoxlove in the previous chapter, because in 1580 the priory's commendator was made the first Lord Blantyre. Now Blantyre has another place of interest, again overlooking the river. This is the National Memorial to David Livingstone, which includes the house in which he was born. This humble dwelling with bare floors is curiously impressive, with its multiplicity of relics of the great missionary and explorer, and its glimpse of firm Victorian purpose on the fringes of poverty proclaims Livingstone's achievement, as the most inspired of sculptured memorials could not have done.

seven

Glasgow
and the Lower Clyde

Glasgow is at the same time one of the oldest settlements in Scotland and one of the newest cities. When Edinburgh was already a walled medieval town with castle and palace, Glasgow was still that 'beloved green place' which is believed to be the meaning of her name. This, not nineteenth-century philistinism, is the reason why so little that is really old survives in the city. The city of Glasgow is the creation of men of boundless energy and inventiveness, with the raw materials within reach and the means of export at their doors, and their epic achievement is in its way as impressive, even as romantic, as the dramatic contrast between the old and the new towns of Edinburgh.

Medieval Glasgow may be seen in the course of a single morning. It was little more than a village in the shadow of the Cathedral, a magnificent building the choir and crypt of which date from the middle of the thirteenth century, and which have survived intact. The church is dedicated to St. Mungo, otherwise St. Kentigern, who came here from Culross towards the end of the sixth century to convert the Britons of Strathclyde. An earlier church, consecrated in 1136, was burned down, and the existing crypt and choir were built by Bishop William de Bondington, a stout-hearted prelate who resisted attempts made by Henry III of England upon Scottish independence. Another patriotic bishop was Robert Wishart. Edward I sought to win him over by a grant of oaks for the building of a spire, as well as of stags for his table, but Wishart used the timber for building artillery, and in course of time it was Bishop Robert who absolved the Bruce of Comyn's murder and

placed the crown upon his head at Scone. Externally, the Cathedral is
not notably impressive, but it must be remembered that the western
towers were taken down in 1846. The interior makes a very different
impression. The nave, completed by Wishart about 1300, is of great
height and its central aisle has a timber roof. A very fine stone rood-
screen erected by Archbishop Blacader around 1500 heralds entry to
the five-bay choir. It is however the lower church, commonly called
the crypt, which is the chief glory of the Cathedral, and it is doubtful
if there is another in the kingdom which can match it. This is part of de
Bondington's achievement. One descends a stone stair from the tran-
septs, and the effect of the low vaults and squat columns is dramatic and
moving. The shrine of St. Mungo is gone, but its site is marked by a
raised platform with four columns, near the centre of the area. The
Saint's well is in one of the chapels. Some of the groining of the vaults
is especially effective, and is like branches in a forest of low, dense
trees, particularly intricate above the spot where the altar of the Blessed
Virgin Mary stood. In the Blacader Aisle, which is two centuries later
in date, the masons have obviously copied the earlier carving. There
was a tradition that the Blacader Aisle contained the tomb of St. Fergus,
apparently based on a low relief carving and inscription containing the
name 'Fergus'; but Dr. James Richardson showed in his Rhind Lectures
that the carving contained a play on words and that the legend should
really read: 'This is the aisle of Carver Fergus.' As with almost all
Scottish churches, Glasgow Cathedral has a simplicity and indeed
severity which are part of the original concept and have nothing to do
with despoliation by the Reformers; but it must have possessed rich
woodwork, all of which has gone, and stained glass, which was replaced by Munich glass in Victorian times, which in its turn happily is

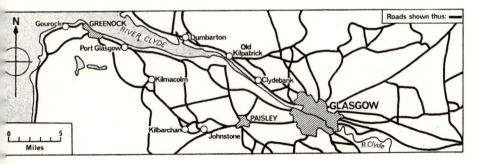

being replaced by contemporary work by such excellent artists as William Wilson and Sadie MacLellan.

Within sight of the Cathedral, in Castle Street, is what is probably the only other surviving fragment of medieval Glasgow, the house known as Provand's Lordship. It is part of the Hospital of St. Nicholas. Later it became the manse of the Provand (Prebend) of Barlanark. It contains some furniture and tapestries, and is hallowed by the tradition that Mary Queen of Scots stayed there when Darnley lay sick of the smallpox near by. But of the remainder of Glasgow's equivalent of Edinburgh's Old Town nothing is left, and the Cathedral is isolated in a desolate setting, the most prominent feature of which is the Necropolis, a cemetery of gigantic proportions the more prominent for being on a hillside.

In the early days, her church ruled Glasgow. The bishops ruled the town in the name of the King. They could make or destroy everyone from the provost down. Even when the Reformation loosed the bond of this domination, prosperity came slowly, because the small university town lay upon a river which faced away from the trade of European ports, and her only really profitable export was based on the rich herring fisheries of the Clyde. The Union of 1707 laid the foundation of Glasgow's wealth, as it opened the way to trade with the American colonies and by the stroke of a pen the Clyde found itself facing in the right direction. In 1727 Daniel Defoe found Glasgow the only Scottish town increasing both in domestic and foreign trade, producing or purveying many goods of sorts not known in England, and selling them cheaply. Defoe, moreover, noted that Glasgow was anything up to twenty days nearer to Virginia than was London, and that her ships did not have to go in convoy for fear of the Channel privateers. Half a century later she had become the greatest tobacco market in Europe, and the Tobacco Lords were her aristocracy, proudly walking the Plainstanes in scarlet cloaks and cocked hats with gold-knobbed canes in their hands, none daring to speak to them unless first spoken to. The American War ended this; but the surge of Glasgow had begun, her boundless energy and teeming ideas were already astir, and she saw at once that in the huge coal and iron deposits of Lanarkshire she had means to win herself a foremost place in the Industrial Revolution. She bred inventors. Bell with his 'Comet' pioneered steam navigation.

Neilson revolutionised smelting through his hot-blast process. And she turned her attention to her modest river, deepening it and equipping it until Glasgow grew into one of the world's great ports.

No one, with this epic story in mind, will feel deprived of historic ruins or elegant buildings. He will want to see the embodiment of the story. The one way to achieve this, although these days it is fraught with the uneasy feeling of involving a backward glance in time, is to sail down the river from the Broomielaw as far as Clydebank. More than once I had the rare privilege of doing this during the war, when as each shipyard loomed up the roar of the riveters swelled and the blue flames of oxy-acetylene torches stabbed the gloomy shadows under the red hulls of every sort of craft from tank-landing ships to aircraft-carriers. There was grandeur in this pageant of the gigantic effort of a single city. There is still grandeur in the procession of tall cranes which mark the line of the river, but the industries which are significant to-day are not so manifestly spectacular, and although the enterprise of Glasgow as a city has not lessened it is dispersed in numberless glass-and-concrete factories and one must accept the old river as its symbol.

The spirit of this enterprising and creative city is, however, vividly reflected in the phases of its architecture. This is something which is far too little realised, perhaps because so many of the examples are scattered instead of presenting themselves in impressive masses as in Edinburgh. For an ordered, chronological summary of examples I recommend the little architectural handbook to the city edited by Professor McLaren Young and A. M. Doak.

The growing town of the eighteenth century is sparsely represented now, yet there is some good material. St. Andrew's Church in St. Andrew's Square is a smaller edition of St. Martin-in-the-Fields, but with a lofty, slim steeple rather typical of the town. It was built about the middle of the century by Allan Dreghorn, but its most remarkable feature is the plasterwork of the barrel-vaulted ceiling, which springs from slender, fluted Corinthian columns of great elegance. The Adams did several things in Glasgow. Robert's two great pieces were the old Infirmary, now replaced, and the Trades House in Glassford Street, the exterior of which is still fine although modified a little and sandwiched between tenements. More interesting than either, perhaps, is Pollok House, at Pollokshaws, designed by William Adam and therefore dating from quite early in the century. Until a few years ago this was the home of the late Sir John Stirling Maxwell, a great connoisseur and collector who was a pioneer authority on Spanish painting as far as Britain is concerned, and two magnificent El Grecos in the house are relics of this interest. Pollok House, which has many other treasures, including well-known paintings by Blake and some beautiful silver, lies in the midst of extensive parkland, woods and farm-land, although the unseen city surrounds it on all sides. The stables of the house are contemporary with it, but the gateway to the stable-yard dates from about 1600.

The period of planned neo-classical building which may loosely be called Regency, the period which in Edinburgh produced some of her grandest terraces and circuses, in Glasgow coincided with the founding of the city's great industries. As these industries in one way or another depended upon the river, it is appropriate that the first planned development area bordered upon the river, in the Barony of Gorbals. The promoter was James Laurie, and the district became known as Laurieston. The only section completed was Carlton Place, designed by Peter Nicholson, who soon went to London, and it still is a handsome range of buildings, although it seems more elegant in contemporary prints. Laurieston House, in the centre of the eastern portion of the terrace, completed in 1804, has an exceptionally fine interior, worthy of Adam. Blythswood Square is about twenty years later. This would not look out of place in Edinburgh, with its finely balanced blocks and its austere lines relieved by Ionic porticos. William Stark's Courts of Justice in the Saltmarket were rebuilt in 1913, but they are an admirable essay in the Doric style, even if not quite as they were, and the portico appears to have been closely modelled on the Parthenon. A more imposing portico, of the Corinthian order, fronts the old Royal Exchange, now Stirling's Library, a David Hamilton building with superb interior; and the Royal Bank of Scotland behind it, on Royal Exchange Square, presents an Ionic portico of considerable grandeur. For churches, on the other hand, even at the height of the classical revival, Gothic was the only proper manner, and how well they could build in it can be seen in St. David's Church, on Ingram Street, which replaced the eighteenth-century Ramshorn Church. The architect, Thomas Rickman, a Birmingham Quaker, was author of a book on Gothic architecture. As to early industrial buildings, little of worth has survived, but an exception must be made of the extraordinary structure which once was Houldsworth's Cotton Mill, now the Cheapside Bonding Company warehouse. This is a brick building with an iron framework, austerely functional except for lofty pilasters of faintly classical appearance. It dates from 1804–6.

But the real architectural splendour of Glasgow belongs to Victorian times. She is indeed the supreme surviving Victorian city. England built in brick and stucco, materials which crumble and peel. Glasgow built in stone, usually in red sandstone of local origin, and gloomy though it may grow with age it is comparatively indestructible and survives to commemorate the exuberance and aspirations of the men who made the city great. The queasy aesthetic appetites of some modern commentators, enfeebled by too much study of principles and by artistic prudery, have quailed before Glasgow's achievements of that age; but distaste is giving place to a degree of admiration, not only for creative energy in such quantity but for the quality of craftsmanship, which would be hard to match to-day.

The focus-point of this manifestation is the Kelvingrove Park, a wide green space of ninety acres through which flows the Kelvin. The park is dominated by the university buildings on Gilmorehill, a fantastic mixture of Gothic and Baronial designed by Sir Giles Gilbert Scott and completed in 1870. It is a foreign importation. A Glasgow architect might have done it better, but nevertheless it is in keeping with the city of its time and its silhouette is part of Glasgow's. Looking at it, it is hard to remember that this University is a fifteenth-century foundation, its ceremonial mace a Gothic silver piece of the same century, or even that Adam Smith was among its many distinguished teachers. Only the Lion and Unicorn stair and the gatehouse preserve portions of the earlier college. It possesses, incidentally, in the Hunterian, by far the most interesting university museum in Scotland, the collection of Dr. William Hunter, who died in 1783. Hunter in his way as a collector personified Glasgow, for he combined an omnivorous taste with shrewd judgment. His cabinet of medals was one of the best in Europe. His huge library contained many priceless volumes. His insect collections were arranged by Fabricius. His scientific exhibits range from anatomical preparations to palaeontology. And in addition the paintings which he brought together include works by Titian, Rembrandt,

Veronese and Jan Steen. The Hunterian's archaeological collection is specially rich in relics of the Antonine Wall. On the opposite bank of the Kelvin, in a red sandstone palace of the very last year of Victoria's reign, is the municipal art gallery and museum. It contains the richest art collection in any gallery in Britain other than the national ones in London and Edinburgh. It has excellent examples of the Italian, Dutch and Flemish schools, and a superb range of the French school. Its armour collection, the gift of Scott the shipbuilder, is unrivalled outside London. And the Burrell collection—the gift of another shipping magnate—when eventually displayed will be found to contain tapestries, stained glass and oriental textiles and ceramics which few museums on either side of the Atlantic could hope to excel. As much as any buildings in the city, these collections on Gilmorehill and at Kelvingrove are monuments to Glasgow's energy and generosity.

The West End of Glasgow is in many respects architecturally comparable with the West End of Edinburgh, although not many people will believe this. Perhaps buildings in Glasgow tend to be finished just a little less perfectly, and there is no doubt there is more grime and more neglect here, but there is a great deal of splendour too. Opposite Gilmorehill and on the left bank of the Kelvin the park rises steeply to the one-time mansions of Park Terrace, which fronts an entire neo-classical quarter. In the centre of it is Park Circus, designed about the middle of the century by Charles Wilson. It has been called with justification perhaps the grandest town-planning enterprise in mid-Victorian Britain. Wilson a little earlier had carried out the earliest of the Great Western Road terraces, Kirklee Terrace, a dignified and beautifully proportioned straight run. Charles Wilson again is responsible for the oddly impressive Trinity College, which dominates this area with its enormous campanile and twin towers. But the whole of this district and as far west as Hillhead is full of good things, and a leisured walk through its streets and crescents is recommended for a summer evening, even if some of the house-fronts have grown shabby and the sound of students' radios are sometimes strident.

The climax of the classical revival in Glasgow came with Alexander Thomson, better known as 'Greek' Thomson. He was an original, one who was no mere copyist of ancient temples but who had such a profound sympathy with their principles that he could achieve striking new effects by their means. His first church was the Caledonia Road Church of 1856–7, in which an Ionic portico is dominated fantastically by an enormous Italianate tower. It gives the impression of being much larger than it is, and in an American city might have been carried out on a colossal scale. The well-known St. Vincent Street church of two years later is one of the great monuments of its time, similar to the earlier church in concept, but subtly far different, with a beautiful tower in which classical discipline contrives to control strange details topped by a vaguely Indian pinnacle. His famous terraces—Great Western Terrace, Walmer Crescent and Hyndland Road—are all disarmingly simple essays which set and solve whole series of little problems, such as an illusion of curves where no curves actually exist. But Thomson could be quite as convincing in his use of Egyptian or oriental detail. His Egyptian Halls in Union Street is a purely commercial warehouse, but even the garish modern shop-fronts applied to its street floor do not destroy the quality of the Egyptian colonnade and projecting eaves. A rather different colonnade treatment marks the Grosvenor building in Gordon Street, on top of which J. H. Craigie dumped a sort of Greco-Roman temple forty years later.

In some respects, Glasgow's addiction to classicism is more marked than Edinburgh's. For churches, Edinburgh tends to stick to gothicism, or at least to put a gothic steeple on a classical frontage, but Glasgow has several churches which are as near to Greek temples as the Madeleine in Paris. St. George's-in-the-fields, with its Birnie Rhind pediment sculptures, is perhaps the best of them. However, the architecture which I feel truly reflects the bustling extravagance of late nineteenth-century Glasgow is mainly in the field of commercial buildings, and sometimes verges on the preposterous. John Burnet's Italian Gothic Stock Exchange in Buchanan Street is a good example, and in another vein so is McGibbon's Florentine palace of a warehouse in Tradeston Street. The strangest of all those Italianate buildings is Templeton's carpet works on Glasgow Green, a fantasy by William Leiper carried out in stone and brick and tiles with its skyline of notched crenellations sticking up like footlight-masks on an early Victorian stage. But sheer monumentalism overlaid with eclectic and costly detail is the main characteristic of this period in the city. It can be very good. The St. Andrew's Halls, an astonishingly early work by James Sellars, shows just how good it could be, and it will be a tragedy if this building, recently gutted by fire, cannot be rehabilitated. Appropriately enough, the City Chambers are in this manner. Externally they are not unsuccessful, but the interior, with its extravagance of materials, achieves only a pomposity which I should say is quite untypical of the Fathers of this of all cities.

At the end of the Victorian age Glasgow's interest in the arts matched her industrial and commercial precocity. Until the 'eighties, she was as philistine as any other British city devoted to expanding commercial interests; but for some years a group of painters had been pursuing a vigorous, independent line and discussing their views in the studio of W. Y. McGregor, and when the Glasgow Institute capitulated to them the city's wealthy merchants decided they might be worth patronising. They were open-air painters like the Barbizon school in France and the Newlyn group in England. They conceived of everything in terms of pattern. Rich colours and bold painting were what counted with them, not the transference of intellectual concepts into story pictures in the Victorian tradition. But if they were denounced as heretics by some of the Edinburgh critics, it may be this quality which appealed to the self-made men of Glasgow, for Glasgow began to buy the paintings of 'The Boys', and before long they were being hailed by Continental critics and bought by Continental galleries.

Special fame abroad, however, was reserved for the architect member of the group. The Germans especially, enthused by Hermann Muthesius, hailed Charles Rennie Mackintosh as the pioneer of the new functionalism in architecture, the apostle of northern romanticism in a world dominated by the classical ideal. Where the classicist thought first and last of a faultless façade, Mackintosh began with the room beautiful and made the walls and roof a mere enclosure and expression of the rooms within. Mackintosh was indeed a significant figure, and the architecture of modern cities at the same time owes him a debt and forgets the lessons which he taught. He in his turn admitted the debt he owed to the buildings of the vernacular tradition in his own country. The Mackintosh building which all Glasgow knows is the School of Art. It is hard to credit that this building dates from a mere decade after the City Chambers. The interior is an essay in the style of Art Nouveau, with which Mackintosh was linked particularly through his interior

21   *Glasgow Cathedral: the Crypt*

decoration and furnishings. Miss Cranston's Willow Tea-Rooms in Sauchiehall Street were equally typical.

Recently I looked across the city from the top of the fourteen-storey technical school building whose flatiron shape looms above George Square. From such a point Glasgow loses all character, since everything fades into insignificance against the grouped tower blocks which have risen in the Gorbals and elsewhere. All the character left is concentrated in the giant cranes which mark the line of the Clyde, trailing off dimly westwards to the last great grouping at John Brown's yard at Clydebank, cradle of the Cunarders. The extraordinary thing about the epic of the Clyde is that in size it is quite an insignificant river, no greater than the Tweed which rises in the same hills. The making of the river might be dated from 1662, when there was 'ane little key builded at the Broomielaw'; but a century passed before Glasgow faced up to the fact that her sea-borne trade began twenty miles down the river and had to be reshipped to her warehouses in wherries by way of a channel which could be waded across at low tide. The man who really laid the foundation of Glasgow as one of the world's great ports was John Golborne of Chester, who by dredging and building rubble jetties so confined the river that it scoured out its own channel to a much greater depth. Later, both Rennie and Telford had a hand in the work. But in 1840 the Town Council handed over its responsibility in the matter to the Clyde Navigation Trust, who began their splendid stewardship of the river by grandly rebuffing interference first by the Lords Commissioners of the Admiralty and then by a body of 'gentlemen from a distance' trying to centralise control of British harbours in London. What they made of the river might to a stranger, especially in November murk, look like a nightmare scene of docks and sheds and dirty water; but it has been fecund dirt, and out of it has grown not only prosperity but a great tradition which has caught the imagination of such as Kipling and Muirhead Bone.

The north shore of the lower Clyde is both interesting and attractive, a sort of shelf of Lowland territory overhung by foothills of the Highlands. Its most prominent feature is Dumbarton Rock, a mass of basaltic material rising right on the shore and dominating both the land passage and the river. It has been a stronghold since early times. Although it lay just beyond the westernmost fort of the Antonine Wall at Old

22 *Culzean Castle, Ayrshire*

Kilpatrick, the Romans do seem to have occupied it for a time in the fourth century, no doubt to deny it to their enemies, who might otherwise have been in a position to outflank them across the river. The name, however, means 'hill of the Britons'. It is as the capital of the Britons of Strathclyde that it became of the first importance, and it appears to have been the Alcluith of Bede. Ossian refers to it as Balclutha in telling the story of Moina, daughter of the King. Fingal mourns

> I have seen the walls of Balclutha, but they were
> desolate . . .

That they were indeed strong walls one can infer from Bede, who records that Alcluith was the most completely fortified place possessed by the Britons. They were built up again many times and in many forms between perhaps the twelfth century and the sixteenth, but little of the old works can now be seen. Wallace endured imprisonment in Dumbarton before he was carried to London and execution. Indeed, this is probably how the sword in his monument at Stirling, already mentioned, came to be associated with his name, because for centuries it had lain in Dumbarton Castle. There is a sundial given by Mary Queen of Scots, who stayed in the castle for a few days in 1548 before embarking for France, but the most remarkable incident involving the place in her reign was its capture by Thomas Crawford of Jordanhill, who scaled the rock with a party of soldiers during the dark from the seaward and steepest side and without loss captured the Archbishop of St. Andrews and the French Ambassador together with the entire garrison excepting only the Governor, who escaped by fishing-boat, rather ungallantly leaving his wife behind.

The south bank of the Clyde below the Broomielaw presents as unpromising an appearance as any dockland area. Govan, two miles downstream, with its towering shipyard gear and its tenements, looks the picture of nineteenth-century industrialism, and it is hard to credit the old prints which show it as a pretty riverside village, far less the claim that 'it has often been likened by strangers from the south, to Stratford-upon-Avon, the birth-place of the immortal Shakspeare'. However, Govan kirkyard contains some very remarkable monuments from a remote past. They are sandstone blocks of various shapes and sizes, most of them weathered so badly that in some cases it is hard to discern what they have been; but a few are in reasonable condition, especially a sarcophagus with relief carvings of scenes from a stag-hunt alternating with panels of interlaced work. This stone in particular resembles slabs at Meigle, in Perthshire, and other places. Those slabs are Pictish work, and the country of the Picts is the north-east. In the west one expects to find strong Irish influence. Only on the sarcophagus is the carving comparable in quality to north-eastern work, and one is tempted to wonder if the sarcophagus was not brought from Perthshire and its detail later imitated on the other stones. There seems to be no doubt that there was a strong settlement hereabouts in the early Christian period, because a few miles west along the main road, at Inchinnan, there are more carved stones. Most of the way along this south bank of the river, none the less, is uneventful from the antiquary's point of view, despite the fact that it must have been well tenanted since the Middle Ages, and although Renfrew became a royal burgh under David I it has nothing whatever to show having historical associations.

As the river opens out into a wide estuary opposite the Rock of Dumbarton, the south bank contrasts more and more sharply with the mountainous background to the northern shore. Port Glasgow with its shipyards and factories links on to Greenock, where the natural deepwater channel begins. Greenock, until little more than a century ago, was Scotland's premier port. The sea is at her doorstep, and to it she owed her prosperity. In 1800 she led Scotland both in shipbuilding and in shipping tonnage. Next in importance in her golden age to her seven ship-yards were her seven sugar refineries, fed by a harvest brought her by the sea. The inventions of her most illustrious son, James Watt, were to revolutionise the propulsion of ships, and by preying upon ships her most notorious son, Captain Kidd, laid up his pirate treasure beyond the Atlantic. Indeed the long-held privilege of Greenock as a deepwater port, fought so hard for by Glasgow, brought a bitterness greater than that of a pirate's victim. The privateers who attacked Napoleon's merchant-vessels brought riches to the town, and Greenock's own merchants did much to break the monopoly of the East India Company. Now the anchorage off Greenock is little more than a stopping-place, famous though that is in all the seven seas: the Tail of the Bank. The town's tragedy is that only the sea can bring her prosperity, for her

back is to a wall of hills and moorland which offers her no room for
industrial expansion.

The high moors and hills behind Greenock form a wind-break for the
lower lands to the east. They are fertile lands, and were extensively
developed in the Middle Ages, much of the country being owned by
the monks of Paisley Abbey. Later, the damp and relatively mild climate
encouraged the development of textile manufactures, and weaving
early became the basic industry. A few miles south-east of Port Glasgow, at the foot of Strath Gryfe, is Kilmacolm, and whether one takes
the Lochwinnoch or the Paisley road from here the way is through
villages and little towns which have been built upon the loom. In
Kilbarchan the National Trust has preserved the cottage of an eighteenth-century hand-loom weaver, looms, furnishings and all; while at
Houston, a few miles to the north, is a model village of about the same
period. Paisley, however, is the town in which it is possible to learn
most about Renfrewshire in a short time.

The town of Paisley has grown around the Abbey Church. The nave
of this is used to-day as the parish church, but this is only a remnant of a
very fine early fourteenth-century church, which replaced a twelfth-
century one founded by Walter Fitzalan, Lord High Steward of Scotland, destroyed by Edward I. The west front is especially impressive.
The doorway is deeply recessed and rich in its effect, with a beautiful
five-light window above. On the south side of the church is a chapel
dedicated in 1499 to St. Mirren, the patron saint of the town, now used
as a burial-place for the Abercorn family, once probably an oratory for
the monks. There are some sculptures illustrating the life of St. Mirren.
Some of the sculptures of the wall corbels are among the earliest in
Scotland, dating from the first half of the thirteenth century. Other
corbel sculptures of early fifteenth-century date are remarkable for
their quality and variety. There are several royal tombs in the church,
and there is an effigy traditionally associated with Marjorie Bruce,
daughter of King Robert, who was killed while hunting at Knock Hill,
close to the town.

In the Abbey Church is a bronze statue of Robert Tannahill, chief
among the remarkable group of versatile weavers produced by the
town. These weavers of the early nineteenth century were independent
men, owning or hiring their own looms and paid by the piece, so that

their time was their own; and their thoughts while weaving strayed through many fields, from botany to poetry, generally inspired by the lovely countryside around what was then a rural community. Several of the weavers, among them a direct ancestor of the present writer, published very fair verse as well as political lampoons of a radical nature, and Tannahill's verse, in the vein of Burns, attained considerable and deserved popularity.

Paisley was, of course, famous for its shawls, and anyone interested in their history and manufacture is recommended to visit the burgh museum in High Street, which contains the most complete collection of these shawls in the world. The shawl was not a product of original artistry, but was rather the result of ingenious mechanical imitation of Turkish and Indian materials which flowed into this country after Napoleon's explusion from Egypt in 1801. Kashmir shawls were the favourites and brought high prices, and the Paisley weavers were determined to imitate them on the loom. The 'pine-pattern' which is typical of Paisley work is directly borrowed from the Kashmir shawl. Paisley caught the fashion, and for fifty years in Scotland it was normal for a bride to be 'kirked'—that is, to attend church for the first time with her husband—wearing a Paisley shawl.

eight

Ayr and Ayrshire

It is a mistake to think of Ayr and Ayrshire primarily as the Burns Country. It is all too easy to explore this part of Scotland with a Burns anthology in one hand, identifying place after place referred to in the verses. The guidebooks encourage this sort of thing. The trouble is that Ayrshire is not a country with arresting natural features, or with spectacular ruins, and a visitor can easily find himself on a literary paper-chase, seeing only what preoccupied the poet. The world appeal of Burns—and one of the best renderings of *Tam o' Shanter* which I have heard was in an after-dinner speech by a Chinese—stems from the fact that he was of the earth earthy—

Kyle for a man, Carrick for a cow

—as the ancient rhyme of those parts has it; and more than once it has been remarked that the most glorious view in Ayrshire, the sight of the Arran peaks floating in molten gold across the waters of the Firth, receives not a single mention in all the works of Burns.

The best part of the town of Ayr is the district near Wellington Square, much of which must date from the second quarter of the nineteenth century. These houses are not of course on the scale of contemporary buildings in Edinburgh or Glasgow. Most of them are only a couple of stories high, but their stonework, warmed by a summer sun, is a pleasure to linger over, with here a well-turned pillar, there an elegant porch. The dominant building in the Square is the County Offices. This is a handsome group designed by Robert Wallace about

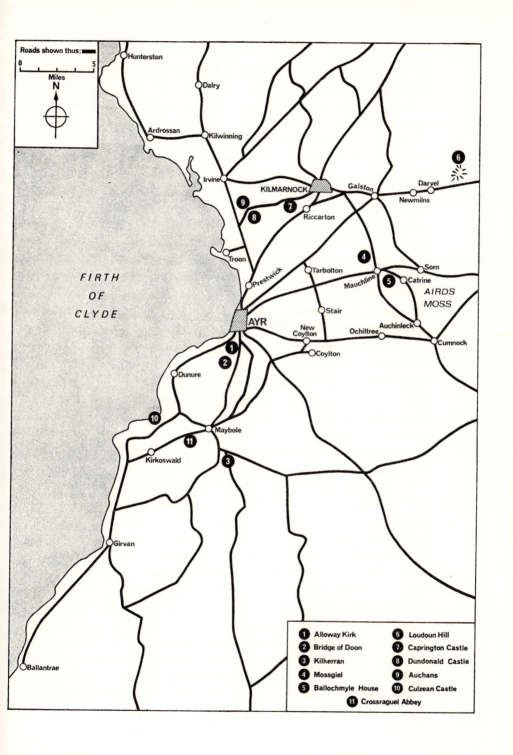

Roads shown thus:

0 _____ 5
Miles
N

FIRTH
OF
CLYDE

Hunterston
Dalry
Ardrossan
Kilwinning
Irvine
KILMARNOCK
Galston
Darvel
Newmilns
⑨
⑧
⑦
Riccarton
Troon
Prestwick
Tarbolton
④
Sorn
Mauchline
⑤
Catrine
AIRDS
MOSS
Stair
AYR
New
Coylton
Ochiltree
Auchinleck
Cumnock
①
②
Coylton
Dunure
⑩
⑪
Maybole
Kirkoswald
③
Girvan
Ballantrae
⑥

① Alloway Kirk   ⑥ Loudoun Hill
② Bridge of Doon   ⑦ Caprington Castle
③ Kilkerran   ⑧ Dundonald Castle
④ Mossgiel   ⑨ Auchans
⑤ Ballochmyle House   ⑩ Culzean Castle
⑪ Crossraguel Abbey

1820, said to be modelled upon the Temple of Isis in Rome, the columns of its portico cut from Arran stone. Facing the columns is an enormous monument to the thirteenth Earl of Eglinton. He it was who organised the celebrated Eglinton Tournament in 1839, a full-scale medieval pageant laid on in the park of his castle near Irvine. Armour, tabards, pavilions were made in quantity, lances turned, swords forged. Lady Seymour, grand-daughter of Sheridan, was appointed Queen of Beauty, and among knights who entered the lists was the Emperor Napoleon III. But, for the west of Scotland, August was a bad choice of month. The Tournament ended in a downpour, tempers were lost, and the only happy outcome I know of is the gigantic silver presentation piece depicting knights and their ladies with manifestly early Victorian features which is deposited in the hall of the County Offices.

The older parts of the town are harder to find, as they have been eliminated or overgrown by commercial developments. Both Romans and the Britons of Strathclyde had settlements here, as numerous finds show. Ayr had its first charter at the start of the thirteenth century, from William the Lion, and at the other end of the century Wallace burned down—with its inmates—a barracks built by Edward I and known as the Barns of Ayr. The existing Wallace Tower is a nineteenth-century monument, perhaps on the site of an earlier structure; and the only building which might perhaps date back to this time is the Auld Brig which Burns used in his poem of *The Twa Brigs*, a high, narrow structure of four arches, massively buttressed, traditionally built with money given by one of two maiden sisters who saw her lover drowned at the ford here when the Ayr River came down in spate. The New Brig, 150 yards down-river, was put up about 1785 to a design by Robert Adam. However, it fulfilled the prophecy in Burns's poem when it was reduced to 'a shapeless cairn' by a flood, and had to be rebuilt in 1877. The harbour at the river's mouth sheltered a busy traffic in the early nineteenth century, exporting something like 50,000 tons of coal alone from the Ayrshire mines; but the seaport has dwindled to modest dimensions, and Ayr has exchanged the creak of rigging for the howl of jets by day and night out of the great air-terminal at neighbouring Prestwick. The town which Burns knew around the Twa Brigs, with the 'lofty and picturesque' houses described just after his time, has gone. Ancient features such as the castle besieged at the time of Haakon's

invasion have completely gone; but Stewart Cruden remarks on substantial remains of Cromwell's Citadel, visible near the harbour and
other places, but surviving in plan at least among papers in the Library
of Worcester College, Oxford. This Citadel was a purely alien im-
position, one of five built by Cromwell to hold down Scotland and
carried out by a German engineer. It was a powerful fortification, large
enough to contain a market-place, so it is not surprising fragments have
survived. It embraced the twelfth-century church of John the Baptist,
where Robert Bruce held a parliament in the year after Bannockburn,
and Cromwell turned this into an armoury, paying in compensation a
mere £150 towards building the Auld Kirk. The Auld Kirk, which contains three of the old guild lofts, is the church were Burns was baptised.

The Burns legend cannot long be overlooked in Ayr. It begins in the
High Street, at the Tam o' Shanter Inn, a perfectly genuine survival,
complete with thatched roof and sign, yet inevitably looking self-
conscious in a street full of the stench of motor traffic and invaded by
commercial stores. The universality of Burns' appeal lies in the fact that
his poetry is rooted in the common events of life, indeed in the common life of a countryside which bred plough-horses rather than poets.
A friend of mine who is a distinguished critic has called him a good
minor poet. It took me precisely thirty seconds to find the reply to this
one in the pages of Burns himself—

I care not, not I—let the Critics go whistle!

Burns can indeed afford to toss aside attempts to lessen his stature, because so many generations in so many countries have responded to the
warm appeal of his humanity, where sonnets in studied, classic mould
would leave them cold and once-praised epics merely sound to them
pretentious. But the very readiness of his appeal has of course brought
vulgarisation upon him, and then commercialisation, and his image is
prostituted on the hoardings. In spite of it all, a pilgrimage from the
Inn along what is more or less the route of Tam's notorious ride, ending at Alloway kirk two miles to the south, can be strangely moving,
because no moonlit ruin ever inspired a Wordsworth to such extravagance of invention or to such infectious flow of words and rhythms as
this bucolic countryside inspired in Burns. Kirk-Alloway 'whare
ghaists and houlets nightly cry' is an empty shell, but so it was in the

poet's day. The cairn 'where hunters fand the murder'd bairn' is in
fact a prehistoric burial-cairn which did contain human remains. Almost the whole poem is in fact splendidly documented, and one is left
with a ready appetite for the numerous Burns relics in the museum by
the cottage where the poet was born. The cottage, before it was preserved, came into disrepute for a time as an alehouse, then went
through an even stranger period as 'a temperance refreshment room'.
By the Auld Brig o' Doon, scene of the poem's climax, is the Burns
Monument, surely the most unsuitable memorial ever raised to anyone,
designed by Thomas Hamilton in the style of the monument of Lysi-
crates in Athens! In this Grecian shrine, which might have served for
Keats, are preserved such intimate relics as Jean Armour's wedding
ring and the bibles given by Burns and Highland Mary to one another.
A primitive monolith, with druidic outline, would have been far more
significant, for Burns drew constantly upon local superstition and based
even a poem like *Tam o' Shanter* on a gruesome local legend of the
Carrick country.

The 'landed gentry' have at all times played a leading part in the history of Lowland Scotland, and this is especially true of Ayrshire. Sir
James Fergusson of Kilkerran has underlined this in his *Lowland Lairds*.
The relationship between laird and ploughman has frequently puzzled
readers of Burns, who see effrontery in a 'peasant' addressing—and
publishing!—a passionate poem to a lady glimpsed only once, the
Bonnie Lass o' Ballochmyle. But in Lowland Scotland there is an intricate web not only of close relations, but of actual kinship, linking the
great houses with the lairds, and lairds with burgesses, and all these
with what would in England be called the yeomen on the land, and this
is something which Burns constantly reflects and which makes it easier
to understand how he could leave his plough and be accepted in the
notoriously critical drawing-rooms of Edinburgh. A good sampling of a
cross-section of Ayrshire, then, can be had by heading south through
Maybole to a point where one may see Kilkerran on its rising ground,
then turning north-west along the fringe of the hillier country to
Cumnock, returning to Ayr by Auchinleck, Ochiltree and Stair.

Kilkerran is a monument to the 'improving' lairds of the eighteenth
century, who tackled the backward state of agriculture in Scotland and
within two or three generations made Scottish farming the envy of

other countries. Afforestation was the first step taken at Kilkerran, and some of the original trees planted in 1706 are still there. Productive land was extended by judicious purchases and by the taking in and liming of moorland. Farmers were persuaded to abandon their conservative, wasteful methods of working. And in addition to putting heart into the land, the lairds found time for devoted public service, in Parliament or on the Bench, and would often put their hands in their purses to enable, for example, a son of the parish minister to train for a career. And readers of Burns should keep in mind that a laird like Sir Adam Fergusson, well travelled, well read, Member of Parliament for the county, spoke the doric as broadly as Burns spoke it. These lairds, indeed, had the strength and energy, both of body and of mind, which Robert Chambers in 1826 noted as typical of Ayrshire. The lairds of Auchinleck were the same. Old Auchinleck, the judge, had no time for the foppish manners and mincing speech which his son, James Boswell, introduced from London; but one cannot read the *Journals* without concluding that 'Bozzy' was at least as tough as his father, and that the qualities which Ayrshire soil bred into the Clydesdale strain passed also into Boswell's blood. Auchinleck built himself a fine new home at the time of the 'improvements', as happened at Kilkerran, although Dr. Johnson affected to prefer the ancient family castle, now in ruins. Ochiltree, which lay on the other side of the Lugar Water and is now demolished, was neighbour and rival to Auchinleck in the Middle Ages. Ochiltree had associations with John Knox, who married the seventeen-year-old daughter of the family in 1564, and with Claverhouse, who married Jean Cochrane, presumably in the successor to the older castle, burned down in 1680. In the village, incidentally, is a cottage to be noted in passing as the birthplace of George Douglas Brown, who wrote *The House with the Green Shutters* as a counterblast to the sentimental Kailyard school of writers—a sombre masterpiece, in which Ochiltree becomes the grim village of 'Barbie'. Much more attractive is the village of Stair. It lies on a lovely stretch of the River Ayr, and has the look of what it has been, a community serving and served by a long line of able and conscientious lairds. These too have included great public figures. Viscount Stair, who in 1682 published his *Institutions of the Law of Scotland*, was one of Scotland's greatest legal writers. Even here there are Burns associations, for the poet apparently kept the housekeeper amused while his friend Davie Sillar paid court to the housemaid, Peggy Orr.

An interesting circuit may be made by setting off first on the road to Mauchline. This in the beginning is even more of a Burns pilgrimage than the way to Alloway. Tarbolton is not the most pleasing of Ayrshire villages, but Burns constantly made visits there to meet a convivial company, and the Bachelors' Club which he and his friends formed there in 1780 is now preserved by the National Trust. They made fun of some of the villagers and one of these, the tailor Saunders Tait, tried to vilify the poet in verse. Five miles on is Mauchline. This is a very different village, and was almost on Burns's doorstep when he farmed at Mossgiel. This was his home when he wrote 'The Jolly Beggars', 'The Cottar's Saturday Night' and indeed virtually the whole of the Kilmarnock Edition, and Mary Morison, Holy Willie and Poosie Nancy and a dozen others lie in the kirkyard. But Mauchline is in country which has always teemed with stirring events. Traditionally, this is the country of Old King Cole, and a horn preserved in Caprington Castle, near Kilmarnock, is associated with his name. Coil or Coilus, if he existed, must have been a chieftain of the Britons of Strathclyde who resisted the Picts and Scots. The name lingers on in Water of Coyle and Coylton, and possibly indeed in the name of the whole district, Kyle. Mauchline also had its martyrs in Covenanting times, as a memorial testifies. And in the nineteenth century Mauchline was the centre of a cottage industry, the making of treen, or small woodware, especially snuff-boxes. The companion volume to this, *The Highlands*, refers to the boxes made at Laurencekirk, and the principle of the wooden hinge used there was used also at Mauchline. There is a tale that this was first devised by one William Crawford of Auchinleck, and that the process was carried to Cumnock and elsewhere; but Mauchline won chief repute for the boxes, a great many of which were decorated with incidents from Burns's poetry or with scenes from the rural life of the region, occasionally with a slightly naughty slant reflecting the same kind of earthy humour which delighted the poet and his readers. The boxes are beautifully made, snugly fitting and lined with foil, and many carry the maker's name.

From Mauchline the road winds past Ballochmyle House, by Catrine where Burns 'dinner'd wi' a lord' in the house of Professor Matthew

23   *Kirkcudbright: the Castle from across the Dee*

Stewart, father of Dugald Stewart, and on to Sorn. At Sorn one may go straight north to Galston, or climb by the Ayr through Aird's Moss to the moors about Muirkirk, thence across the shoulders of the hills in the general direction of Loudoun Hill, a landmark for many miles. This second route takes in two battlefields, Drumclog, where Claverhouse was routed by two hundred Covenanters under Hackston of Rathillet when he tried to disperse one of many conventicles held among these lonely moors, and Loudoun Hill itself, where in 1306 the Bruce won a victory over the Earl of Pembroke and laid the foundation of his ultimate success in the War of Independence. Following the Irvine river, the way lies through Darvel and Newmilns, noted for their laces and muslins, and then after a few less attractive miles, Kilmarnock. Kilmarnock is now a prosperous commercial town of some size, fitting into the county's reputation for textile manufactures by its production of carpets and shawls, but there is nothing to suggest it is a town of past note except the red sandstone monument which reminds us that from a press here in 1786 came the first edition of Burns's poems. However, there are historic places in plenty within miles. To the north, for example, is Dean Castle, superbly restored by Lord Howard de Walden, containing a collection of armour and arms of high quality, and a few miles on, Rowallan Castle is a beautiful example of the medieval fortress beginning to emerge into a mansion in the sixteenth century. To the south are Caprington Castle, already mentioned as the home of the Old King Cole horn, Riccarton, where Wallace spent much time as a boy, and ruined Dundonald Castle on its hill, where the first and perhaps the second of the Stewart kings died. Dundonald is a typical tower-house of the fourteenth century, with a fine hall, its vault enriched by decorative ribs. Dr. Johnson found something comical in this castle, but he was not a connoisseur of archaeological remains.

Kilmarnock is in the Cunningham 'province' of Ayrshire. Another journey may be taken into Cunningham, following the coast road. It passes within a mile or two of Dundonald, and nearer still to Auchans, said to have been built with stones from the Dundonald ruin. Auchans too was visited by Johnson, to meet that former queen of Edinburgh society and notable beauty, the Countess of Eglinton. Allan Ramsay had inscribed his *Gentle Shepherd* to her in her heyday, and she presented the manuscript to her learned visitor from London. Three miles on lies

24 *Paisley Abbey: the Choir*

Irvine, a town of many church spires on the River Irvine where it enters the sea with the Garnock. There are plans for developing the Irvine area, plans for making it one of the 'new towns', but this ancient royal burgh created by Robert the Bruce in 1308 has still in parts a certain atmosphere. Even here there are Burns associations, but the town's own especial writer is John Galt. Galt died in 1839 and is little read these days, but his books have the character and mellow quality of the prints of his day and present a facet of old Ayrshire as surely as the verse of Burns does. Irvine is the 'Gudetown' of *The Provost*. And the Irvine both of Galt and of Burns was the chief centre of one of the most charming of old Scottish crafts, Ayrshire white needlework. Here again is a cottage industry. The linen base for the embroidery would be woven in the village, the wives and daughters of the village did the 'flooerin' (flowering) in their own time, and the motifs used were drawn largely from the plants and flowers of garden and hedgerow, instinctively stylised in the most exquisite taste as by any oriental craftsman. The women met in one another's homes, sitting around a single lamp. Even children could earn something by threading the needles. In Irvine there were as many as 2,000 women needleworkers. The craft became commercialised in time, with stamped patterns distributed and finished 'pieces' later collected and sent to Glasgow for making up, but the best of the mutches and babies' caps and christening robes were the creations of the local women.

Two miles north of Irvine, Eglinton Castle, a romantic structure of 1798, now lies derelict among policies which were planned as one of the 'improvements' of the eighteenth century. Beyond is Kilwinning. The name means the church of St. Wynnin, an Irish missionary of the sixth century, and the town has grown up about the Tironensian abbey founded about 1160 by Hugo de Morville, Constable of Scotland, who also founded Dryburgh. The abbey was cast down—these are Knox's own words in his *History*—by the Protestants of the West under the earls of Arran, Argyll and Glencairn. It is now a ruin, closely beset by a housing scheme, but still impressive, and the wall of the south transept with its rose and lancet windows, its detail simple but beautifully contrived, give some idea of the quality of the building. There were three towers joined to the nave by arches, an unusual feature in a Scottish church. The east doorway retains some carving, and one capital with a pair of figures is Norman in feeling, but the rain and salt winds off the Firth have weathered away the detail. The abbey seems to have been colonised by monks from Kelso. Kilwinning is now spared, by a by-pass, most of the heavy coastal road traffic which used to jam its narrow, twisted street. This leads on through rather built-up country to the port of Ardrossan, and then through more rural surroundings to small water-ing-places such as Fairlie, by way of Hunterston. At Hunterston, vast notices proclaim the entrance to the nuclear power-station, whose twin glass-clad towers now balefully dominate the channel between Green Point and the Great Cumbrae; but the most interesting thing which Hunterston has given us is now one of the treasures of the National Museum of Antiquities—the wonderful brooch found in one of these fields in 1826, an eighth or ninth-century masterpiece of the Scoto-Irish school scarcely less fine than the famous Tara Brooch in Dublin. On the back are scratched two Runic inscriptions showing it had been in the hands of Norsemen. In the Dark Ages the Norse descen-ded constantly upon this coast, until in 1263 Alexander III defeated Haakon at the battle of Largs, the spires of which modern town can be seen across the water to the north.

The coast road south out of Ayr is rich in interest, especially in its earlier stages. There is a crop of castles, or ruins of castles, hereabouts: Greenan, Newark, Dunduff, Dunure. Dunure is now perhaps chiefly remarkable because of the tale that in 1570 the Earl of Cassilis there roasted the Commendator of Crossraguel Abbey over a slow fire until he signed away his lands. Crossraguel is well worth a diversion from the coast road by Maybole, from which it lies a couple of miles to the south. The abbey is guarded by a strong gatehouse and a keep-tower, evidence of the need for defence here between a great tract of wild hill-country and the sea. The church itself is long and narrow, with a typically Scottish three-sided apse. In the chapter-house, the groin vault is carried on a single, central pier. The nave had been closed off, perhaps because the number of monks decreased at the end to only eleven, when the coming of the Reformation permitted local bullies like Cassilis to assert themselves against a church at bay. Yet these Cluniacs hung on until 1592. An interesting feature of the abbey life was that the abbots of Crossraguel had the right to possess their own mint. In complete contrast to this embattled abbey of the fifteenth century, less than three miles away on the shore are the mock battlements of Culzean Castle, a Gothic fancy built for a later Earl of Cassilis by Robert Adam in the 1770's, now the property of the National Trust. Set behind a formal garden with here and there a sub-tropical tree, beyond a park with woodland walks, Culzean is built on a rocky headland plunging straight into the sea and tunnelled with smugglers' holes known as the Coves of Culzean. Externally, this is very unlike an Adam house. No doubt the architect was guided by the ancient Kennedy stronghold which preceded it. But the castle possesses one of the loveliest of Adam interiors. The plaster ceilings have been restored and re-coloured, from original moulds preserved in Ayr. Special features are the oval staircase, exquisitely contrived, and the round drawing-room with furniture and carpet designed for it. The finest views from the castle are from the flat presented to General Eisenhower for his lifetime as a mark of esteem from the Scottish people.

nine

Dumfries and Galloway

Dumfries and Galloway form a region of exceptional variety. Bleak uplands and hill tarns contrast with rich pasture-lands and pretty villages. And as men have found it good from early times, it is also rich in antiquities and bygones. One may fittingly, therefore, make the hub of one's exploration not merely Dumfries itself, but the Observatory Museum on its hill in the Maxwelltown area of the town. This museum always reminds me of the Outlook Tower in Edinburgh. This is not simply because it possesses a camera obscura. The real parallel derives from the questing spirit which seems to lurk there as the ghost of Patrick Geddes lurks in the Outlook Tower, although in Dumfries the eye which stays the Wedding-Guest is alight with the spirit of a different sort of dedication, a dedication to antiquities of every sort and size. There is no streamlined display here, no subtle lighting of selected objects in the modern manner; but few local museums have combed the countryside so thoroughly as Mr. Truckell's.

Dumfries is neither so appealing nor so obviously possessive of a long past as some of the smaller towns of the region. It has become a considerable industrial centre, especially since the last war, and there is a good deal of overspill into the pleasant country on its fringes. The local red sandstone, too, while somehow it adds to the character of a medieval building, as a rule looks much less happy when shaped into the alien modes favoured by the Victorian builder. From the Observatory one can see the Midsteeple of the Town House, one of the few older buildings, but although this bears the date 1707 it has not the charm of the vernacular town houses. Some older stones are incorporated in the building, including the Royal Arms and a St. Andrew in the western wall, which may have come from the sixteenth-century prison. A number of buildings survive from later in the eighteenth century. These include several associated with Robert Burns: the house in which he died, where many personalia are preserved, St. Michael's church where he worshipped, and the Globe Tavern, where he pursued the convivial life which he had led in so many village howffs in Ayrshire. His tomb, where his wife Jean Armour also is buried, rivals the monument at Brig o' Doon in unsuitability, and would certainly have drawn a quatrain from Burns himself, that master of satirical epitaphs. In spite of its lack of old buildings, however, Dumfries is an ancient town. The principal material evidence of its age is to be had from what remains of the old Castle of Dumfries, now nothing more than some ditches and mounds over which the house of Castledykes has been erected. The castle seems to have been in existence in the twelfth century, when the town was created a royal burgh by David I. Edward I captured it in 1300. Bruce seized it after his murder of the Red Comyn in the Greyfriars Monastery in February, 1306, the act which sealed his resolution to champion Scottish independence. But the only medieval structure in

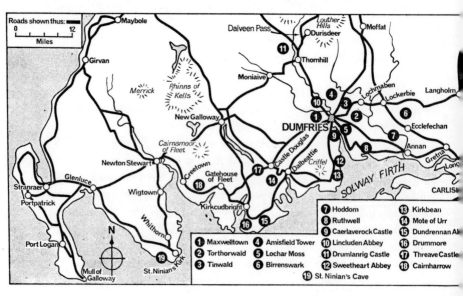

the town which still survives is the Old Bridge across the River Nith, joining Dumfries to the Stewartry of Kirkcudbright. Its nine arches were reduced to six at the beginning of the nineteenth century, but it remains one of the most impressive medieval bridges in the country, and is still perfectly sound although used now only for foot passengers. The arches are by no means uniform, either in size or in shape, and at the western end the parapets are out of alignment, and altogether the bridge has a natural grace very difficult to achieve in an age enslaved to precision. Tradition attributes the bridge to Devorguila, widow of John de Balliol and foundress of several religious houses in the neighbourhood as well as benefactress of the Oxford college founded by her husband, and some of the best authorities have accepted this tradition; but the Royal Commission on Ancient Monuments quotes from a papal letter of 1431 which refers to the building of a bridge 'recently begun over the river Nyth near the Burgh of Dumfries'. A spate wrecked a portion of the bridge in 1620. This was rebuilt within a year.

Of many relics in the Observatory Museum, I will mention only two, as they are associated with old or vanished buildings in the town. One is a bell believed to have come from St. Michael's Church. It is inscribed in Latin in Lombardic letters: 'William of Carlyle, Lord of Torthorwald, caused me to be made. In honour of St. Michael, A.D. 1443.' This must be one of the oldest church bells in Scotland. The second item is the celebrated Dumfries Siller Gun. This little silver piece has been altered and now has the form of a barrel fitted with a comparatively modern stock, but it once possessed a wheeled carriage, broken in 1808. An inscription on the gun gives the date 1589; but the gun came to the town in 1617, when James VI stopped on his return to England and was entertained by the Provost and Town Council in the Painted Chamber of the Town Clerk's house. The King presented this miniature gun to the incorporated trades of the town, to be competed for at an annual wapinschaw—one of those repeated efforts to induce the burghers to improve their marksmanship instead of indulging in golf or football.

Dumfries is not very centrally placed for journeys up and down the lands bordering the Solway, but there is a particularly heavy concentration of places of interest in its neighbourhood. A one-day circuit to the east of the town can yield a cross-section of regional history not easily rivalled in this island. Crossing the Lochar Moss by the A.709 one comes first to Torthorwald, then by moving north on a side road to Tinwald: names which betray the penetration of Danes and Norsemen here in the Dark Ages. They came by way of Ireland, and swarmed on both sides of the Solway. The emerging kingdoms of England, however, surging up from the east, from their side also came to Annandale. Indeed this small corner of Scotland facing across to the English shore of the firth was to be hotly contested for many centuries, because it lay athwart the main route to the north through the hills. It knew not merely raiders, but the tramp of great armies, and so its strong places had to be very strong. The Tower of Torthorwald is not a great castle, but even in its present ruinous state its strength is evident. Carlyle of Torthorwald, donor of the bell, was of the family which probably built the tower in the fourteenth century. A mile or two north of Tinwald is another tower, two hundred years later than Torthorwald, but as remarkable. This is Amisfield, a splendid example of the tentative growth of domestic out of military architecture in the sixteenth century. By contrast with grimmer fortresses of earlier times, Amisfield had certain amenities, crude perhaps but effective. There is plasterwork, some of it coloured; and there is an extraordinary carved oak door, now removed to the National Museum of Antiquities, showing Samson slaying the lion, the hero garbed in the costume of about 1600. A similar tower, rather earlier but probably by the same builder, is Elshieshields, a mile north of Lochmaben. Lochmaben itself had a castle of great strength and size, which Stewart Cruden now puts back in date to the early fourteenth century. It is ruinous, but must have been a redoubtable place. It is set on a promontory in the loch, and walls, scarps and ditches block the land approach. The original fortress belonged to the Bruces of Annandale, but in 1298 it fell into the hands of Edward I, who added a 'peel'. The castle changed hands more than once. Indeed, it is a good example of Bruce's contention that these powerful castles were more important to English invaders than to the Scots, whose strength lay in defence in depth. In the sixteenth century Lochmaben became a Maxwell seat. When James VI came against the traitorous Lord Maxwell in 1588 he needed only two days to reduce the castle by means of cannon.

The number of cairns and hill-forts, hut-circles and lake-dwellings

shows that the coastal strip along the Solway was populous in early times. In the early years of our era this was the home of the Selgovae, a Celtic, apparently Pictish tribe, who were of the Gallgaidhel, or 'stranger Gaels' from which the name Galloway is derived. Agricola came against the Selgovae, probably in the summer of A.D. 79. He seems to have pressed on right through Galloway to 'that part of Britain which looks towards Ireland', in the words of Tacitus. On the other side of Nithsdale, perhaps six or seven miles from Lochmaben and on rising ground, is some important evidence of the Roman invasion, probably Agricola's. This is the group of fortifications on the hill of Birrenswark. There have been many theories about these, but the layout of at least some of them strongly suggests Roman military engineers, and there is plenty of evidence to show the Romans occupied the site for a long time, including coins and Samian ware and stones with inscriptions referring to the Emperor Hadrian and to the Second Cohort of Tungrians and to the famous Sixth Legion. Some of the most interesting finds were a considerable number of leaden sling-bullets which the Romans called *glandes*. The most sophisticated discovery, however, was not Roman but of native workmanship: a beautiful bridle-bit of bronze and enamel, with flowing Celtic lines, now in the National Museum of Antiquities.

Birrenswark is only two or three miles north of Ecclefechan. Here in a house known as the Arched House Thomas Carlyle was born. His father and uncle, who were master-masons, built the house. It belongs to the National Trust and contains furniture from the Chelsea house, personalia and MS. letters. The Sage is buried in the churchyard here, together with his parents. At Hoddom, close by, there are some fragments of a sculptured cross as significant as anything else in this corner of Scotland; but I will resist this small diversion and deal with them presently, together with the much more remarkable related cross at Ruthwell. Meanwhile, I will pursue the main south road to Gretna. Gretna is interesting for more reasons than the one familiar to the tourist. Even its notoriety as the goal of runaway couples is founded on a minor falsehood, for Joseph Paisley who began the marriage business in the middle of the eighteenth century was never the village blacksmith and probably had no experience of the right use of an anvil, although he had tried nearly every other trade. For a century it was a

26   Caerlaverock Castle: interior courtyard

profitable business. Only when Lord Brougham in 1856 brought in the twenty-one-day residence requirement did the stream of candidates dwindle and the post-boys have to be compensated for lost fees. A much more ancient association with law-breaking is that Gretna was on the border of the Debatable Land. This was an area between Sark and Esk which belonged neither to Scotland nor to England, and in which the law of neither was effective. Here gathered numerous ruffians and renegades, among them such celebrated gangs of border rievers as the Armstrongs, but among some of them grew up a sort of Robin Hood tradition, and on the Scots side of the Border at least there was more than a sneaking admiration for such a character as Johnnie Armstrong of Gilnockie, so treacherously trapped by James IV and hanged with his followers. The Treaty of Norham (1550) tried to solve the problem by depopulating the Debatable Land, but two years later it was divided between the two countries concerned. There survives one monument to those troubled days in the shape of the 'Lochmaben Stane', a large boulder near the farm of Old Gretna, not far from the Solway shore. Commissioners from England and Scotland used it as a trysting-place to discuss Border disputes. It is mentioned in early charters, usually as the Clockmabanstane. It seems to have formed part of a stone circle, and it has been associated with the Welsh hero, Mabon, and with a Celtic deity of the same name.

From Gretna to Annan there is a rather monotonous stretch of road with the flat lands and shallow waters of the Solway on the left, but from Annan the road to choose is the secondary one which runs through the *Redgauntlet* country to Cummertrees, then on to Ruthwell. The village of Ruthwell is remarkable for two reasons. The first is the man who was ordained its minister in 1798, Dr. Henry Duncan. He is remembered as the originator of the Savings Bank movement; but this provided only a single chapter in the life of one of those versatile old Scots ministers who could have achieved eminence in a dozen different ways. He aided his little parish by the Solway by practical acts which ranged from the importing of corn from Liverpool to meet a scarcity, to raising and captaining a company of volunteers when Napoleon threatened. He created *The Dumfries and Galloway Courier* newspaper, and his other writings included a four-volume philosophical work. He was no mean draughtsman, sculptor and landscape-

gardener. In his own calling he was elected Moderator of the General
Assembly, yet four years later, so strongly did he hold his views, he left
his church and the manse and garden to which he had devoted so much
care to join the Free Church. Against this background it seems a small
matter that he distinguished himself as a geologist by identifying the fossil
footprints of quadrupeds in the New Red Sandstone of Corncockle
Muir, and even that he left his mark as an antiquary by his description of the ancient monument in his parish celebrated as the Ruthwell
Cross. But the cross is the second remarkable feature of Ruthwell,
because it is one of the most notable early Christian relics in Europe.
It is now preserved inside the church, which is up a side-road from the
village. Rising out of a well contrived in the floor, the cross is a dramatic and splendid thing, seeming to span the centuries between this
modest nineteenth-century place of worship and the dim, early days of
the faith. But the real significance of the cross lies in its sculptures,
which combine the exquisite decorative artistry of the north with the
humanistic ideals of the far-off south. The vine-tendrils on the sides
are reminiscent of the Lindisfarne Gospels, whereas the figure of
Christ is almost Greek in feeling—were it not for the moustache without a beard, a hint of pagan northern tribes. The Rood of Ruthwell may
well commemorate the ascendancy of the Roman over the Celtic
Church, achieved at the Synod of Whitby in 664, and the dominance of
Bernician power over the Celtic fringe, reflected, too, in the sculptured fragments at Hoddom, and in the great cross at Bewcastle over
the Border.

About a mile to the east of Ruthwell is Comlongon Castle. This
fifteenth-century tower belonged to the Murrays of Cockpool, forebears of the earls of Mansfield. The surviving iron yett (gate) should
be noted, as it is a rare feature, because the strength of yetts was such
that in 1606 the Privy Council required them to be destroyed except
in the towers of those Border barons who could be trusted. However,
I will press on beyond the Lochar Water to the ruin of one of the most
splendid castles in all Scotland. Caerlaverock is military architecture at
its noblest. It reminds us instantly of one of the great fortresses of
medieval France. Indeed, its fame reached France, for an Anglo-French
poem of the fourteenth century, *Le Siège de Karlaverock*, describes its
capture by Edward I in 1300. The poem pictures it much as it is to-day,

although it has been rebuilt, evidently early in the fifteenth century. Great double towers dominate the entrance, and there are, or were, towers at the other angles of its triangular plan. Turrets and parapet walks were corbelled out, enriching the walls with shadowed cornices. The interior court is overlooked by great windows of later date, surmounted by carving. The grooves for the portcullis and drawbridge machinery may still be detected, and close by a loophole through which molten lead or quicklime could be poured on men assaulting the entrance defences. The castle was surrounded by a moat and by boggy country, hazardous for heavily armed knights; yet under Edward's personal direction the siege of 1300 lasted only a day or two, so devastating were the siege-engines.

Most of the hinterland of Dumfries and Galloway is comparatively deserted and even rather wild, but an excursion up Nithsdale is rewarding. About a mile north-west of Dumfries the Nith receives the Water of Cluden, and in this beautiful spot in the twelfth century Uchtred of Galloway founded an abbey for Benedictine nuns. Archibald the Grim, Earl of Douglas, suppressed it in 1389 on the ground that the nuns had become disorderly, and founded in its stead a collegiate church, the now ruinous Lincluden, which Dr. Douglas Simpson has called by far the loveliest thing of its kind in Scotland. The fourth Earl of Douglas, that Marshal of France whom Shakespeare praised in *Henry IV*, seems to have built the church, and the tomb of his wife Margaret, daughter of Robert III, one of the glories of Lincluden, is—as Dr. James Richardson remarks—the only surviving royal tomb in Scotland. Heraldry dominates the design of this once-magnificent tomb and is used lavishly throughout the church, notably in the windows of the chancel. There has been some fine figure-carving too. The Apostles from the rood loft are terribly worn, but their draperies have been exquisitely cut. These romantic red sandstones ruins, where Burns often sat, are in the finish of their detail comparable with Melrose and Dunblane.

Nithsdale is Maxwell country. Close to Lincluden stood the Maxwell home of Terregles, rebuilt in its present Georgian style in 1789. At Terregles Mary Queen of Scots had her second-last resting-place in Scotland, after her defeat at Langside. In passing it is worth looking at the 'queir' (choir) of Terregles, a little Late Gothic church containing the tomb of Edward Maxwell, who died in 1568, marked by one of those quaint local representations in execution rather like the Amisfield door. The Maxwells, like Lord Herries who sheltered Mary at Terregles, remained stubborn Roman Catholics, and the fifth Earl was thrown into the Tower for his part in the 'Fifteen. A mile or two further on is Irongray kirkyard, where Scott erected a stone to the memory of the original of Jeanie Deans, Helen Walker. Literary associations abound. A few miles up into the moors to the west lies Craigenputtock, the family farm where Carlyle wrote *Sartor Resartus*, and beyond the Bogrie hill from here is Maxwelton House, where Annie Laurie was born in 1682. Here one may turn west to Moniaive, a peaceful village on the edge of Covenanting country, or east to Thornhill and the passes over the northern hills.

At Thornhill one is back in Nithsdale. Four miles north, glimpsed through rich, wooded, rolling country, is Drumlanrig, its turreted Renaissance splendour in pinkish local sandstone standing out against spacious parks. Daniel Defoe—a good commentator on this part of the country—remarks that 'the Surprize of seeing so fine a Building in so Coarse a Country adds to its Beauty'. Both in plan and elevation Drumlanrig resembles Heriots Hospital in Edinburgh. Built in the last quarter of the seventeenth century by William, first Duke of Queensberry, it cost so much that the Duke spent one night only under its roof and went of to Sanquhar Castle to brood over the accounts while his duchess had to beg the chamberlain for the price of a gown. In 1810 the castle's ownership passed to Henry, first Duke of Buccleuch and Queensberry. The woodlands which Smollett had praised were replanted. The gardens which, to quote Defoe again, were 'like a fine picture in a dirty grotto, or like an equestrian statue set up in a barn', were maintained in even greater magnificence, not only in their formal beauty but in their productivity, so that Lord Ernest Hamilton in the time of the fifth Duke could say 'the piles and pyramids of fruit that crowded the dining-room table at every meal were something altogether outside my experience' Defoe proceeded from Drumlanrig to the Enterkin Pass, which he writes of vividly in his *Journey through Scotland*—'There cannot above two go abreast; and the Precipice is much more dreadful than *Penmanmawr* in *Wales*.' Defoe of course hated hills, and to most eyes to-day the Pass would be sheer delight, with cool springs bordered by thyme and foxgloves and wild violets and the far views to Blacklarg Hill and the Kells. But the easy way across the Lowthers is by the Dalveen Pass, which brings one close to Durisdeer. Durisdeer is a sleepy little village in the shelter of the hills, with a church dating from 1699, worth a visit for some of its sepulchral monuments, which reflect local history. There is a marble memorial to the second Duke of Queensberry, and a more than usually descriptive epitaph to a Covenanter: *Daniel McMichel, Martyr, shot dead at Dalveen by Sir Iohn Dalyel for his adhereing to the Word of God.* . . .

One of the pleasantest pilgrimages from Dumfries is to New Abbey, known more widely as Sweetheart Abbey. The name of Sweetheart (Dulce Cor) derives from the fact that the abbey was founded in 1273 by Devorguila, wife of John Balliol and mother of the 'Competitor' King, to receive her husband's heart, which was laid upon her breast when she came to be interred in the abbey. It was a Cistercian house, and well chosen for site. Sheltered by the mass of Criffel, it is on land well watered and well favoured. Built of local red sandstone, the abbey church itself is nearly complete, apart of course from the roof, and is in Middle Pointed style, dating from the thirteenth and early fourteenth centuries. Although the general effect is rich, decorative detail is not ornate, in accordance with the Cistercian rule. Sweetheart supported five hundred monks, and there was a precinct of about 24 acres surrounded by a high and massive wall of granite blocks, a considerable part of which has survived. Inevitably the abbey suffered by its proximity to the Border, and it became impoverished by the long-drawn-out struggle of the Wars of Independence. But after the Reformation, when the Lords of the Congregation ordered Lord Herries —whom we have encountered at Terregles—to destroy the abbey, he, who had been educated there, refused. The last abbot, Gilbert Brown, died in Paris in 1612. Among many tombstones is that of William Paterson, founder of the Bank of England.

Another local man to die in Paris, 180 years later than Gilbert Brown, was born five or six miles down the road from Sweetheart. The birth took place in a gardener's cottage on the Arbigland estate, close to Kirkbean, and the man was John Paul, to become famous as Paul Jones, founder of the American Navy. He was shipped to sea at the age of twelve from the port of Whitehaven, on the opposite shore of the

Solway, and later was a smuggler between Solway and the Isle of Man. In 1777 he returned to within a few miles of Kirkbean as commander of the American frigate *Ranger* when he landed with a party in an attempt to seize the Earl of Selkirk as hostage for important prisoners in British hands. The Earl was not at home. Lady Selkirk later wrote that the sailors 'really behaved very civilly', and although they took some plate Paul Jones himself bought it and politely returned it to its owners. The gardener's cottage fell into disrepair, but in 1831 Lieutenant Pinkherm of the U.S. Navy left money for repairs. The U. S. Navy presented a memorial font to Kirkbean church. The circuit back to Dumfries by way of Dalbeattie should be extended to follow the Water of Urr to the Mote of Urr. This immense mound, five hundred feet long and seventy-eight high, is one of the outstanding examples in Britain of the type of early Norman fortification known as a motte. The Bayeux Tapestry shows these structures to have been earth-mounds surrounded by a fosse or ditch and crowned by a timber tower at the highest point. The timber towers have entirely gone in all cases, but careful excavation has sometimes revealed evidence of post-holes which confirm the record of the Tapestry.

The length of the Solway coast is deceptive. Dumfries is less far from Edinburgh than it is from the Mull of Galloway, and the only way to savour the many points of interest in these coastlands is to occupy several days in doing so, and preferably weeks. The A.711 provides a straight run across the moors, through the parish of Kirkgunzeon, locally pronounced with the 'z' omitted, a route studded with keeps such as Corra Castle and Drumcoltran Tower. After Dalbeattie the road creeps down the Urr and then follows the coast at a distance. In another sheltered spot like Sweetheart's lies the abbey of Dundrennan, again a Cistercian house, and one of David I's foundations. It is sadly ruined, but there is enough left to spring many surprises, beginning with a rather startling contrast between a Norman exterior and an interior with beautifully proportioned gothic arches. The abbey contains two of the most interesting ecclesiastical sculptures in Scotland. One is the monument to an abbot, a figure which Richardson estimates to be the oldest sculptural representation of a Cistercian in Britain, clearly thirteenth century. More than seven feet high, it seems to commemorate some strange and horrible incident in the abbey's history, for the abbot has a dagger in his breast and his feet are upon the slain body of a kilted man with a dreadful wound in his side from which the bowels protrude, in Richardson's view the man who murdered the abbot. Another monument, a flat slab beautifully carved in low relief, also represents a monk in the habit of the cuculla, surrounded by an inscription which reveals him to have been a cellarer of the abbey in the fifteenth century.

On this coast there are perhaps even more ancient forts than medieval ecclesiastical remains. One of the best forts is on a hill on the farmlands of Drummore, two or three miles south of the main road and overlooking Kirkcudbright Bay. There are three distinct ramparts, and the position must have been a strong one. This no doubt was another station of the Selgovae, and it has been identified by some with the Caerbantorigum of Ptolemy. The estuary which it overlooks narrows northwards, and where the Dee enters the sea lies Kirkcudbright, capital of the Stewartry. This is one of the most picturesque towns in Scotland, from its quay with its occasional coastal steamer or small tanker to its wide streets with gay, multi-coloured houses. It is hard to say how far this gaiety is spontaneous, and how far it derives from awareness that many painters of note have come from this town and its neighbourhood, but there is no doubt that the 'Kirkcudbright School' of painters of the late nineteenth century was noted for its freedom of colour and its decorative sense. The originators of the movement were George Henry and E. A. Hornel, both eventually Scottish Academicians. Henry shocked and excited the country by his 'Galloway Landscape', a significant early painting of the Glasgow School which drew its strength from the Stewartry countryside. Hornel, Australian-born and Kirkcudbright-bred, restlessly fed his appetite for colour as far off as Japan, but he returned to his own town and his house here is now a museum of his work. The rather baffling name of the town—pronounced Kirkoobry—simply means the kirk of St. Cuthbert. Of its very ancient past nothing remains. Even the medieval castle has entirely gone. But the ruined mansion of Sir Thomas MacLellan of Bombie survives, and his massive tomb with effigy and skull-and-crossbones, erected in 1597, is preserved in the nineteenth-century Greyfriars kirk. The MacLellan family was one of those which Charles I tried to win over by coronation honours, and the barony of Kirkcudbright was

bestowed upon it, a title which has died out. The town has a character-istic Tolbooth at the west end of the High Street, with a high tower and stone steps, the date of it probably the same as the Mercat Cross of 1610, formerly in the street but now at the top of the Tolbooth steps. Tradition has it that the tower is built of stones removed from Dun-drennan after the dissolution of religious houses. The ship weathervane above the tower no doubt commemorates Kirkcudbright's former im-portance as a port. An English traveller of 1722 remarks it has 'the prettiest navigable river' he had seen in Britain, with 'a depth of water and room enough to hold all the fleet of England'. After the execution of Mary Queen of Scots—Mary had left Scotland for the last time by ship from Kirkcudbright—Lord Maxwell plotted in Spain with Philip II, advising him that the Invincible Armada should first make for Kirk-cudbright, and Maxwell did in fact land here himself in April, 1588, to muster his tenants and prepare for a Spanish landing, but James VI struck at him with astonishing speed and energy.

Some miles up the Dee from Kirkcudbright, and indeed almost at Castle Douglas, lies one of the most important strongholds in Galloway. Threave Castle, on an island in the river, was built by Archibald the Grim, Earl of Douglas, in the fourteenth century. The Threave has a grim reputation indeed. A projecting granite block above the doorway is known as the Gallows Knob; and in 1451 the eighth Earl, who kept regal state backed up by a thousand fighting men, and who is even said to have coined his own money known as 'Douglas groats', boasted that for fifty years the Gallows Knob of Threave had never been without its 'tassel'. The following year the Earl perpetrated perhaps the most notorious deed associated with the castle. Sir Patrick MacLellan of Bombie lay in its dungeon under sentence of death when a letter of pardon arrived from the King, but the Earl announced he would dine before reading it and meanwhile had the execution carried out. In 1455 James II took the castle after employing against it the bombard known as Mons Meg, now in Edinburgh Castle. The Threave is the property of the National Trust.

The country between Gatehouse of Fleet and Creetown is a pre-historian's paradise. Cairns and standing stones are scattered from the coast right over the top of Cairnharrow to Glenquicken Moor, where there is a stone circle. Perhaps the most interesting remains are those

28 *Threave Castle*

at the appropriately-named Cairnholy, up the glen from the early seventeenth-century Tower of Barholm, which has been identified as the 'Ellangowan' of *Guy Mannering*. Scott knew Cairnholy too, for he pitched Meg Merrilees' gipsy encampment there. There are two chambered cairns here, close together, one of them traditionally the tomb of King Galdus, who is supposed to have given his name to Galloway. It consists of two tall stones, set upright, and a dolmen-like chamber roofed with a huge slab of whinstone. It is said that about a century ago one of the servants of the neighbouring farm turned up some ancient battle-axes here with the plough, and the handle of a Roman bronze urn engraved with the head of the Medusa.

If the country below Creetown is full of prehistoric interest, the Wigtown peninsula is filled with memories of the early church. About the year 385 Ninian, son of a British tribal chieftain, went to Rome. The Pope sent him back to correct the errors prevalent in his native land. He came to Galloway and built a church after the Roman fashion, dedicated to his mentor, St. Martin of Tours, and there on 16th September, 432, he died and was buried with others of the faithful. The place of his mission and death was Whithorn. More properly Whithern, the name derives from the Anglo-Saxon for 'white house', and this in the Latin form Candida Casa is how Bede calls the church which Ninian built. Whithorn became a place of peculiar sanctity in the middle ages, and its pilgrims included Robert the Bruce. The Premonstratensian priory of the twelfth century rose upon a Celtic see of the eighth, and it is the ruins of this priory which we find when we pass under the archway in the main street supported on fifteenth-century pillars and crowned by the Royal Arms of Scotland. The most impressive portion remaining is the Norman doorway of the priory church, with four orders in the jambs and arches, either rebuilt or heavily repaired at some remote time. A V-shaped raggle cut through the arch shows that a porch must have been built against it in a later period. The moving feature of Whithorn, however, is not an architectural one but the sudden realisation that the ground on which it stands preserved its sanctity even through the tide of paganism which swept over the land at the beginning of the fifth century, so that Sir Herbert Maxwell could say in his history of Galloway that Whithorn alone of all the towns of Scotland 'maintained the worship of the Almighty uninterrupted for fifteen hundred years.' Bishop Forbes in his life of St. Ninian recounts the emotion evoked in him by the place, tracing its influence on men through the ages, from the early Irish missionaries to James IV, who came yearly to Whithorn, driven by remorse to put an iron girdle of penance round his waist and to wear it to the day of his death at Flodden. Amid all this, Ninian's own church seemed to have gone without trace. But excavations east of the priory church have brought to light the remains of a very ancient building with a pale plaster on its masonry. This may well be Candida Casa itself. However, there are innumerable relics of early Christianity here at Whithorn, in the shape of carved stones which speak across the centuries with perturbing eloquence. The oldest, and in some respects the most touching, is the fifth-century pillar of indurated claystone inscribed in crude Latin:

> We praise thee Lord. Latinus aged 35 years
> and his daughter of 5. Here the descendants
> of Barrovad made the monument (to them).

But no less challenging in this age of doubt is the little monument of local stone, which once stood by the roadside south of Whithorn. Inscribed in straggling letters LOC STI PETRI APVSTOLI—'the place of St. Peter the Apostle'—its boldest feature is the Chi-Rho monogram, in cross form, which was the symbol of the persecuted early Church and which links Whithorn with the catacombs of Rome.

Most caves associated with great figures of the past can show no proof of their associations, but Ninian's Cave on the shore in Glasserton parish has some evidence substantiating tradition. It was during a visit by Dean Stanley in 1871 that an incised cross was first noticed on a rock at the entrance. Subsequently other crosses were found, deep in the cave, all simply but some quite elegantly done. Most of the cave-floor, too, had been paved with flags, on one of which was rudely cut the inscription

SANCT
NI–P.

The crosses are probably eighth century, but the saint might well have used the cave as an oratory. Kirkmaiden kirk, some five miles along the coast, burial-place of the Maxwells of Monreith, has also clearly been the site of an older church, because there are some very early carved stones there, including a six-foot slab incised with a cross rather of Whithorn type and a broad-bladed sword of the period.

Even the moors north of this point are by no means bare of antiquarian interest, and they contain at least one impressive castle, the restored Old Place of Mochrum, with its variety of crowsteps and its dormer-broken roofs. At the head of the wide stretch of Luce Bay lies Glenluce. Here in 1190 Roland, Lord of Galloway, founded an abbey for Cistercians whom he brought from Melrose. The Reformation seems to have spared it as it is recorded as almost entire in 1646, but now only the chapter-house is complete, a building which dates from 1470. The vaulting ribs spring from a central, moulded pillar with eight moulded shafts and an octagonal capital carved with those delightful fragments of foliage which occur from time to time in Scottish work. In this remote corner of Scotland it is strange to think that the last abbot of Glenluce appointed before the Reformation was recommended for the post by Mary and her husband the Dauphin in a letter dated from the sumptuous chateau of Amboise.

ten

Melrose and the Borders

No part of Scotland is more Scots than the Borders. This is odd. The topography is not dissimilar on the two sides of the Border. Linguistically, there is no sharp demarcation at the Cheviots. But history has welded the Border counties into a sort of buffer state with recognisable identity, and subsequent events have set their stamp on this: literary associations, from the Border ballads which drew pathos and poetry from what might be thought a brutalising life, as Sir George Douglas remarked, to the romantic influence of Scott; a common industry, apparent from the sheep on the green hills to the woollen mills of town after town along the Tweed; and social custom, from the common ridings to dedication to the game of rugby football, which causes village meadows to sprout tall goalposts in a degree found elsewhere only in Wales.

Melrose is a natural centre for exploring the Borders. It is well placed, has characteristic features, and has more than the usual share of amenities. But I would suggest that before examining the town itself we should note how it is virtually encircled by traces of early forts and camps, in which it is typical of large parts of the Border country. Southwards are the three humps of the Eildon Hills. Legend has it that the Evil One clove them in three when challenged to do so by Michael Scot, the Wizard—Scot, whom Dante condemned for ever to look backwards for his attempts to pry into the future, but who was in fact one of the greatest of medieval scholars, and whom tradition has it died and was buried in Melrose. Long before Michael Scot, however, the north-east summit of the Eildons had upon it the remains of the largest hill-fort in Scotland surviving from the Iron Age. It commanded a great tract of country, and the confluence of the Leader Water with the Tweed, and it is not surprising that the Romans erected a signal station here. It overlooks the Roman road of Dere Street, the Saxon term for the ancient way from Tees to Forth, and which proceeded to the great camp north of Melrose, at Newstead, generally accepted as the Trimontium of the Romans on the evidence of the nearby Eildon's triple summit. A visit to Newstead is profitless. Excavations, aided by air-survey, have however built up a fairly complete picture of the camps or forts, and the original work on the site is described by the late Dr. James Curle in *A Roman Frontier Post and its People*. There were forts from the Agricolan to the Antonine periods. The most important finds

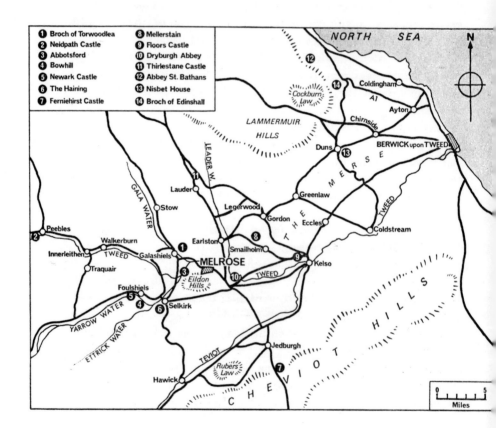

1 Broch of Torwoodlea
2 Neidpath Castle
3 Abbotsford
4 Bowhill
5 Newark Castle
6 The Haining
7 Ferniehirst Castle
8 Mellerstain
9 Floors Castle
10 Dryburgh Abbey
11 Thirlestane Castle
12 Abbey St. Bathans
13 Nisbet House
14 Broch of Edinshall

were a series of altars, which may be seen in the National Museum of Antiquities in Edinburgh. One of the most interesting is dedicated to what has been interpreted as 'the goddesses of the parade-ground', apparently Celtic mother-deities, by the decurion of a legion from Provence.

Melrose is an attractive town, but as it stands of no great antiquity. The market cross probably dates from the sixteenth century, but is too much worn to be very interesting. There are some pleasant old houses near the abbey, but they are not distinctive, and the town owes most of its quality to its situation on the wooded banks of the Tweed and to park-like features such as the Greenyards, surely one of the most delightful rugby-football grounds in the world. It is not difficult to imagine, then, why the Cistercians settled upon this green haugh for their first settlement in Scotland, for they were great farmers and stock-breeders, skilled gardeners and millers. From Clairvaux they arrived in Yorkshire in 1132, and only a few years later they came to Melrose. Records have survived showing how well they husbanded their lands, draining and fertilising them to a standard far ahead of most farmers of their time, and Melrose farmers to-day are probably profiting by their foresight. The monument to the Cistercians' skill and prosperity, the Abbey of St. Mary, has long been ruinous, but even in its ruin it is magnificent.

The original twelfth-century buildings were destroyed by Richard II in 1385. The present church buildings are of the fifteenth century, for the most part, and as the English were in occupation for a good deal of the time it is not surprising to find a strong English feeling, notably in the choir. Other parts of the church are recognisably Scottish—the north transept—but on the other hand there is the celebrated master-mason's inscription which begins—

> JOHN : MOROW : SUM : TYM : CALLIT
> WAS : I : AND : BORN : IN : PARYSSE:
> CERTANLY : . . .

The French form of the name presumably is Moreau. There is French influence in the outer chapels, but as Hannah remarked it is 'without a trace of the Gallic love of soaring forms'. The fabric of a French cathedral tends to be a miraculous piece of engineering in stone, with poise and counterpoise, thrust and counter-thrust contriving one of those lacy, lofty structures which, as in the case of Chartres, may be seen across the level plain long before the roofs of the town about them come into view. French masons or no, Melrose has the more solid solemnity typical of Scotland or indeed of England, and in no way tries to rival the summits of the Eildons. At the same time, more than in any other Scottish church, Melrose is rich in delicate detail, as Scott delighted to describe in *The Lay of the Last Minstrel*, and in that figure sculpture which is elsewhere so rare. The great south transept window could scarcely be bettered by any piece of French flamboyant tracery, and the clustered columns and the carving of capitals are so exquisite as to justify long examination. The foliaceous ornament of these capitals is obviously derived from plants of hedgerow and field, and has all the freshness of invention which follows from this. It is the figure sculpture, however, which is so remarkable to find in a country where most of the 'graven images' have been cast down. For example there is the beautiful piece high on a buttress on the south side of the nave which Dr. Richardson calls 'Our Lady of Melrose'. It is in the tradition of those lovely French Mary figures of the fourteenth century which have both the lissom charm and the inscrutable smile of some Chinese sculptures of the goddess Kuan Yin, but at some time since 1860 the Melrose Virgin has suffered considerable damage to the face. Dr. Richardson believes it just possible that it is the work of a Scottish sculptor. At the apex of the east gable is a Coronation of the Virgin group with associated figures, and these again although much damaged and weathered are of notable quality. But there are numbers of other figures of saints, equally good, in their canopied niches, and there are vaulting-bosses and label-stops in the form of heads too numerous to note but often of marked individuality and character, as in the case of the striking little Moor's head in the Abbey Museum. The museum has a fascinating collection of such fragments. It is in the Commendator's House, a fifteenth-century house about fifty yards distant from the abbey, which at one time was the *palatium*, or palace, of an abbot.

From Melrose to Galashiels is a pleasant four miles by the banks of the Tweed first, then along the Gala Water. Galashiels is in strong contrast to its neighbour. On a grey, wet day especially, its mills give it a rather grim appearance. It is, nevertheless, the more typical Border

town, and is the very capital of the great Scottish woollen trade, scattered though that trade may be throughout the country. Industry to-day tends to be a rootless thing, neither springing from the soil nor yielding returns in terms of personal satisfactions to the workers, which is probably the basic reason for most of our labour troubles; but the Scottish woollen industry is in a more ancient tradition. The Galashiels Weavers' Corporation had its origin in 1666. The facts that the mills of this and other Border valleys possess the most modern machinery and that their products have captured the most sophisticated markets on the Continent and in America do not mean a break with tradition. It is true that Gala Greys and Gala Tweeds were solid, homespun cloths for practical use, but they had enduring quality and drew their virtue from sheep-breeding skills developed by the monks of the great abbeys such as Melrose. The plain weaves of older times were subtly elaborated, textures and colours caught the public fancy, and somewhere around 1840 the old word 'tweel' was transformed into the new word 'Tweed', perhaps because the fame of this Border river on whose banks the woollens were woven had spread into every household in the pages of the Waverley Novels. Galashiels' share in history is interwoven with her products. The Scottish Woollen Technical College is her university, teaching not techniques only but also the philosophy of design. The town's only really ancient house, Old Gala House, she has with practical good sense turned into an art centre, which many years ago the writer had the privilege of declaring open. The oldest part of it seems to date from 1583, to judge by the armorial panel of Andrew Pringle and his wife, and the seventeenth-century wing contains a good painted ceiling, while the eighteenth-century drawing-room has a beautiful plaster ceiling.

At Torwoodlea, two miles north-west of Galashiels, is an interesting relic in the shape of one of the only two or three brochs in the south of Scotland. The wall survives only to a height of a couple of feet, but this in itself is interesting because the work of destruction seems to have been done by Roman soldiers, for whom the broch was probably a challenge. A mass of Roman pottery was found in the ditch, which convinced Dr. James Curle that the structure still stood in the first century A.D. Clearly this must have been a collision-point between the Iron Age broch people, centred on the far north of Scotland, and the

Roman outposts which flowed and ebbed across the Border country. One curious feature was the discovery of a burial-cist containing the remains of a local woman apparently interred with care during the process of the broch's demolition by the Romans.

The winding road by Tweed through Walkerburn and Innerleithen to Peebles is uneventful, so far as obvious monuments are concerned, but beautiful at every turn, especially in spring and autumn. Mills again are the reason for the first two villages' existence. Both have mills with names of world repute, and the second possesses a spring which is probably the original of St. Ronan's Well. Peebles is also a mill town, but it is one of the oldest royal burghs in Scotland, and Fordun credited it with being the cradle of Scottish Christianity. Most of its familiars regard it as just a pleasant little residential town, but it has ancient features, such as the fifteenth-century bridge over the Tweed, widened in modern times, and the seventeenth-century Cross-Keys Inn in which, under the name of Cleikum Inn, Scott housed Meg Dodds. The Tontine Inn was much frequented by parole prisoners from the armies of Napoleon, who performed the plays of Molière and Corneille there and generally made themselves popular in the town, the surgeons among them even assisting the local practitioners. One of these local practitioners of only a year or two earlier was Mungo Park, the great African explorer. By long repute Peebles is one of the most favoured corners of Scotland, sheltered from the scourging east winds; but I feel it supports the objectivity of my views about our declining climate to learn that on 23rd, 24th and 25th June, 1853, the thermometer at Peebles reached 103 degrees in the shade!

A mile or two beyond Peebles, on a knoll in a bend of the Tweed, is Neidpath Castle. A goat's head on a coronet on the keystone of the gateway of the courtyard proclaims the ownership as the Lords Yester, Earls of Tweeddale, and below the stone is the emblem of the original owners, the bunch of strawberries (fraises) from which the Norman family of Fraser took its name. The original Border peel-tower grew by later accretion into a powerful structure, reduced by Cromwell's troops, but improved again after the Restoration when the family arms were set above the gateway. In 1686 Neidpath passed from the Tweeddales, to pay off their debts, to the Duke of Queensberry, who gifted it to his son, the first Earl of March. With the profligate third Earl began the decay of the castle which had served as a summer residence, and his son, fourth Duke of Queensberry, completed the ruin by selling the magnificent timber of the estate, an act which drew from Wordsworth the sonnet which begins—

Degenerate Douglas! oh, the unworthy Lord!

Beyond the castle one may cross the Tweed and return to Melrose mainly by way of the south bank of the river, a much quieter and more leisurely road. Where the Quair comes down to the Tweed lies Traquair House. This is possibly the best surviving example of the organic nature of Scots vernacular building, for its three periods blend faultlessly and indeed to the lay eye appear to be completely uniform. The lands of Traquair were part of the royal hunting forest from the early Middle Ages, and many royal charters were issued from Traquair; but the earliest portion of the building itself, the ground floor of the central block to the west of the doorway, cannot be much earlier than the beginning of the fourteenth century. The house now contains many relics, and the library is quite rich in rare works. There is a table cover reputed to have been stitched by Mary when she stayed here with Darnley in 1566. The road to Melrose passes by ruined Elibank Tower and by Ashiesteel, a house dating originally from 1660, where Sir Walter Scott, between 1804 and 1812, probably wrote *Marmion* and *The Lady of the Lake*.

From Melrose, a short afternoon can embrace both Darnick Tower and Abbotsford. Scott, from his interest in the Tower, was sometimes known as the Duke of Darnick. It is not open to visitors, but is worth mentioning as an excellent example of a sixteenth-century peel-tower. Abbotsford, on the other hand, is a piece of architectural eccentricity. It reflects faithfully the spirit and mind of Sir Walter. Scott was an assiduous but not a scientific antiquarian, and so the house that he built for himself follows no Scottish style; yet the very fact that it derives from so many sources and succeeds in fusing all its parts into a romantic feature of the landscape which he chose for it is of the essence of the great and generous man who put it here. From his boyhood days he had known the site and been familiar with its historic associations. He transformed the undrained meadow deservedly known as Clarty Hole into a laird's mansion and policies. He went to stay there in 1812, but the first part of the house was not completed until six years later. It became, in effect, the first essay in that Romantic, but not unimpressive style termed Scottish Baronial. It contains features modelled upon many originals: for example, the porch of Linlithgow Palace and details of Melrose Abbey. It contains too a considerable number of original fragments, such as a sixteenth-century lintel from Niddry's Wynd in Edinburgh, the door of the old Edinburgh Tolbooth, and a panel dated 1668 probably from the Guild House of the Soutars of Selkirk. Scott was a tireless collector. Everything he collected was evocative. As a result Abbotsford, apart from its associations, is in itself a museum. The armoury contains some fine pistols, including a superb dag by John Campbell of Doune and relics of Waterloo which Sir Walter himself collected on the battlefield. Napoleonic relics include the Emperor's pencase and leather-bound blotter, well-documented pieces both. The sword believed to be the great Montrose's is not so documented, but is a magnificent arm in its own right. Once one of the gems of the collection, the wonderful Celtic bronze chanfrein or horse-mask found at Torrs, was disposed of many years ago to the National Museum of Antiquities. The core of the house is, of course, Sir Walter's study with its desk and plain, workmanlike, easy-chair and in fancy the threads of all Border history seem to be drawn together here.

A much longer foray from Melrose may be made by following the road past Abbotsford to Selkirk. There is a temptation to diverge across the Ettrick Water and to take the road to St. Mary's Loch, at least as far as Newark Castle, first passing Bowhill, a mansion belonging to the Duke of Buccleuch which contains many great works of art, both paintings and pieces of decorative art. Newark Castle is across the Yarrow from Foulshiels, birthplace of Mungo Park. 'Newark' is simply 'new work', to distinguish it from an older fortress, but it is a typical medieval Border keep-tower of the early fifteenth century. Like Traquair across the hills, it was a royal hunting seat, but it became a Scott stronghold, and it was here that the Last Minstrel sang his Lay to the Duchess of Buccleuch.

Selkirk is a pleasant town set on a height, with a triangular market-place at its centre. It is another woollen town, with many mills, but with no particular historical features, although in 1119 a colony of

Benedictines from the region of Chartres came to found a monastery and were diverted to Kelso. It was a royal burgh by the fourteenth century. The wool trade is ancient, but the most important craft in the burgh seems to have been the shoemakers, who are said to have retrieved some of Scotland's honour at Flodden by capturing an English standard and were famed as the Soutars o' Selkirk. On the outskirts of the town is The Haining, a Palladian mansion of the early nineteenth century, although begun by Mark Pringle of Haining in 1794. Out of Selkirk the road climbs over the hills to Teviotdale and Hawick. Hawick is a more extensive town than Selkirk, more commercial in appearance, famed for its knit-wear since the late eighteenth century, but its largely modern High Street possesses one fragment of the medieval town embedded in the Tower Hotel, a former house of the Queensberry family. In the tower of this is all that is left from the conflagration of 1570, which occurred when the citizens, to escape from the English, tore the thatch off their roofs and set it alight in the streets to make a smoke-screen. The earliest structure in the town is the mound known as Hawick Mote. Finds of pottery and a coin of Henry II in its ditch point to a twelfth-century date, when Richard Lovel, a Norman lord from Somerset, held the place. Most of the other surviving relics of the town's past lie in the museum in Wilton Lodge, close by the river. These include a number of medieval fragments, some of them from the vanished St. Mary's Church; but the most ancient objects in the museum are the Roman bronze vessels from a hoard found on Rubers Law more than a century ago. Among them are saucepans and portions of a jug once inlaid and plated with silver. They have been dated to the late second century.

Rubers Law is a hill to the south of the Jedburgh road, a few miles out of Hawick. It was a haunt of Covenanters, who used one of its crags as a pulpit. Turning south after the hill is passed, then north-east again to the Jed Water, one comes to Ferniehirst Castle, an almost complete mansion of the sixteenth century. It has been considerably modified since the first building was put up around 1490, which is not surprising since the English captain, Dacre, of Surrey's army seized it in 1523 and threw it down, and the French laid siege to it in 1549 and another English army destroyed it in 1570. In 1593 James VI decided to destroy it again because it had harboured the Earl of Bothwell. A good deal of modification took place in the seventeenth century, but the early character of the house has survived. The Kers of Ferniehirst have also been associated with the fine old bastel house in neighbouring Jedburgh, known as 'Queen Mary's House', but the Royal Commission dates this house only from the last quarter of the sixteenth century. It is now a museum, and relics associated with the Queen of Scots are preserved in it. Among them is a brass cannon which she is supposed to have presented to Sir Thomas Ker, and undoubtedly it carries the arms of France and Scotland with a monogram which could denote Mary and the Dauphin Francis. Jedburgh possesses many other old houses. It also has a magnificent sixteenth-century bridge of three spans, adjoining the Canongate. But the crowning possession of Jedburgh is of course its abbey. This is built on a site which must have been consecrated to worship from early times, and the abbey museum contains evidence of this in a portion of a sarcophagus of about A.D. 700 carved in a style reminiscent of the Ruthwell Cross, and also various Anglian fragments. A church seems to have been founded here in the ninth century, but the abbey is the work of the Augustinians and dates mainly from the twelfth century. The western façade and the south door are Norman. The Transitional nave is unexcelled in Scotland. Hannah drew a comparison between its modest scale and that of Amiens, but pointed out how relatively rich its mouldings are. Here in 1285 the ill-fated Alexander III married Ioland, daughter of the Comte de Dreux, with gay pageantry described by the chroniclers, but a figure of Death mingled in the masque and there was foreboding because the bride had been destined for a convent, and in a few months the King fell from the cliffs of Kinghorn and the three-hundred-year war with England began. The abbey itself lay full in the path of the English invasions, and both Surrey in 1523 and Hertford in 1544 did terrible damage.

An easy half-hour from Melrose by way of Earlston brings one to a mansion which is among the most elegant in Scotland, Mellerstain. The property of the Earl of Haddington, it is a neo-classical building completed by Robert Adam towards the end of the eighteenth century, but probably begun by his father for Lady Grizel Baillie, the song-writing daughter of Sir Patrick Hume of Marchmont who married the son of the patriot, Robert Baillie of Jerviswood. A few miles to the south-east, close to Kelso, is Floors Castle. Floors must have been begun at about the same time as Mellerstain. It was designed for the first Duke of Roxburghe by Sir John Vanbrugh, or so it is thought. A century later it was remodelled by W. H. Playfair, then working on Heriot's Hospital, and in some details it resembles the Edinburgh school; but the traditionally massive concept of Vanbrugh is preserved, superbly placed to face across the Tweed to the Cheviots. These two fine Georgian mansions give grace to one of the most interesting country towns in Scotland. Kelso has an oddly French air about it. This is specially true of the market-place, although it is difficult to analyse one's feeling. The town is full of character, and has several interesting buildings: the octagonal church of 1773, Walton Hall, the Regency bungalow built by Sir Walter Scott's printer, John Ballantyne, and above all Ednam House, overlooking the Tweed, built in 1761 by a Kelso architect with a London practice, James Nisbet. Ednam House looks across to Rennie's fine bridge across the Tweed, erected to replace an older bridge destroyed in the flood of 1797. The glory of the town, however, lies in its abbey. This is another of the foundations of David I, begun by the Benedictines around 1128. It is unlike any of the other abbey churches, and here again there is that Continental look, a vague memory of Italy in the towers and Romanesque arches. Indeed in its complete state it appears to have had a marked resemblance to Italian originals, for a document of 1517 in the Vatican archives draws some comparisons. Kelso was a very rich abbey, by Scottish standards at least. Records show that the monks almost doubled the yield of their lands during the thirteenth century, by wisdom and good husbandry, and their church reflects their efforts. But noble though it is in its ruin, Kelso Abbey is cruelly defaced. It suffered more than any of its sister houses at the hands of the invaders, and in 1545 Hertford actually declared his determination 'to rase and deface this house of Kelso'.

We complete the circuit to Melrose by making for St. Boswell's, then Dryburgh. St. Boswell's is a market town named after Boisil, in the words of Bede 'a priest of great virtue and of a prophetic spirit', who was sent by Aidan and founded a monastery at the bend of the Tweed known as Old Melrose. The old name of the town is commemorated in Lessudden House at the north end of the town, a sixteenth-century house remodelled in the time of Charles II for the Scotts of Raeburn.

Dryburgh Abbey lies only just over a mile north of St. Boswell's. Dryburgh is distinguished for a number of reasons. It was the first Premonstratensian abbey in Scotland, founded in 1150 by the Constable of Scotland, Hugh de Morville, whose uncle was one of Becket's assassins. It has the most complete and characteristic range of conventual buildings in Scotland. It is the burial-place of Sir Walter Scott and of Lord Haig of Bemersyde. But perhaps above all it appeals to the average visitor because of the sheer loveliness both of its setting and of the ruins themselves, screened from the outside world by great forest trees, its peace broken only by the chatter of finches and the cooing of pigeons. The abbey church is reduced to the high south transept gable, the west front with Romanesque doorway, the east aisle of the north transept and a few associated fragments. The west front doorway is actually fifteenth-century in date, and Dr. Douglas Simpson cites it as an example of the persistence of the round arch in Scottish Gothic. A great deal of the surviving fabric is, however, of the late twelfth and thirteenth centuries. The chapter-house has survived intact, with its stone bench on which the monks sat to hear the reading of their Rule, and there are traces of twelfth-century painted decoration on the barrel-vault. Dryburgh suffered the usual depredations by English soldiery, and Hertford did not fail to pillage it in 1544. But the last monk at Dryburgh did not die until 1600, and Dr. Simpson does well to remind us that the Reformers, far from driving out the monks, actually pensioned them and permitted them to live on in the conventual buildings, here at Dryburgh and elsewhere. The abbey now belongs to the nation.

The last expedition from Melrose which I will describe, and the last in this book, appropriately is within sight of English territory for much of the time. It is to the rich farming region between Lammermuirs and Tweed known as The Merse. I suggest for a start a deviation up Lauderdale as far as Thirlestane Castle. The original castle was built in the sixteenth century by John Maitland, Chancellor of Scotland; but the present turreted mansion was a modification by Sir William Bruce about 1670 for the Maitland who had become Duke of Lauderdale, the the last-named member of Charles II's notorious 'Cabal'. To this period belongs the magnificent plaster-work in the first-floor rooms, perhaps unequalled in Scotland. Charles Edward stayed here after the battle of Prestonpans. From Thirlestane, it is little longer to break away from the

31   *Mellerstain House: the Library*

main roads and go by way of Legerwood. The chancel of Legerwood church is one of the most striking pieces of Norman work in this part of Scotland, with a fine arch springing from carved capitals. Here again as at Dryburgh there are traces of painted decoration of the twelfth century. Greenlaw, a few miles to the east, is less interesting for any monuments of the past than as a survival of an ancient 'vill' of a manor or barony, its small farmer population largely unaffected by industrial or commercial developments, which lends the town a distinct atmosphere of its own. From 1696 until 1853 it was the county town, but eventually Duns took over this honour. Duns, too, is very much an agricultural and market town. Its most notable link with the ancient past is its claim to be the birthplace of Duns Scotus. Strategically it was important, as possession of it was considered to command The Merse, but in the sixteenth century it cannot have amounted to much as in Hertford's day it is recorded as 'a very simple and peevish town'—if Hertford's treatment of it would certainly justify a certain peevishness! Duns is a junction for several nearby worthwhile objectives: to Abbey St. Bathans, in the thirteenth-century church of which is the tomb of a nun with a crozier indicating that she was a prioress, to Nisbet House, a mansion probably built by Sir Alexander Nisbet of that ilk early in the seventeenth century, in which the surviving early feature of defensive shot-holes contrasts with sophisticated plasterwork of the Adam period. But by far the most interesting feature of the Duns district lies at the foot of Cockburn Law, at its north-eastern side. This is the broch of Edinshall. Brochs belong primarily to northern Scotland, and this is the only one within sight of England, or at least within easy reach. Ninety feet in diameter, it is exceptionally large, with a central court about fifty-five feet across. Built inside an earlier fort, its drystone walls, surviving to a height of about five feet, show superb construction.

The extreme point of this journey through The Merse is reached at Coldingham, near St. Abb's Head. Although only a mile from the great sea-cliffs, Coldingham's sheltered little valley was well chosen by the Benedictines who built the priory here on the site of a nunnery of which Ebba, aunt of King Egfrid of Northumbria, was abbess, destroyed by Danish marauders in A.D. 870. The restored choir has become the parish church, but the original portions, particularly as seen in the interior, are in typical and very beautiful First Pointed style. Externally, the arcading between the buttresses is delicate and rather lovely late Norman work. The capitals of the columns are specially to be noted for their use of leaf-forms. They are compared by Dr. Richardson with a 'flourish of tail pieces in a contemporary illuminated missal', and he considers the architectural treatment unparalleled in Britain. Some interesting cross-slabs are preserved at Coldingham, in which the design is drawn in bare outlines with a plain Latin cross and a sword of 'knightly' type with slightly depressed quillons. Coldingham, like the other houses, suffered by the sword in all phases of its history, from its plundering by King John in 1216 to its attempted destruction by raiders in the invasion of 1544. It came under the jurisdiction of Durham until the fifteenth century and its priors were Englishmen; but in 1509 it was transferred to the see of Dunfermline, and its last prior was Alexander Stewart, a natural son of James V.

Index

The numerals in bold type refer to the *figure numbers* of the illustration